Picture Perfect Parties

Annette Joseph's

Picture Perfect Parties

Stylish Solutions for Entertaining

photography by

Deborah Whitlaw Llewellyn

RIZZOLI
NEW YORK

New York · Paris · London · Milan

For Frank,
Alex, and
Levi

First published in the United States of America in 2013
by Rizzoli International Publications, Inc.
300 Park Avenue South
New York, NY 10010
www.rizzoliusa.com

© 2013 Annette Joseph
Photographs © 2013 Deborah Whitlaw Llewellyn
Food styling by Marion Cooper Cairns
Assistant food stylist: Emily Vann

Design and editing by Pinafore Press
Additional photography:
Frank Joseph, page 90
Lesley Graham, page 223

2013 2014 2015 2016 / 10 9 8 7 6 5 4 3 2 1

Distributed in the U.S. trade by Random House, New York

Printed in China

ISBN-13: 978-0-8478-4103-5

Library of Congress Control Number: 2013938941

contents

FOREWORD 6

INTRODUCTION 8

ELEMENTS OF A PARTY 17

Spring Garden Party 27   SPRING

An Easter Lunch for Family & Friends 41

Cinco de Mayo Party 55

Memorial Day Cookout 67

Italian Spring Feast of Squash Blossoms 77   SUMMER

Palio Celebration 89

Summer Pool Grill-Out 101

Fourth of July Picnic 111

Retro Riviera Party 123

Wine Harvest Party 137   FALL

Sunday Supper 149

Thanksgiving Celebration 159

Holiday Cocktail Open House 171   WINTER

Comfort Food Get-Together 183

The White Party 195

Game Day Pizza Party 205

INDEX 216

SOURCE GUIDE 222

ACKNOWLEDGMENTS 223

We try to entertain. We really do. We invite friends over, food is prepared, and we eat. It's usually pretty straightforward fare with the basics of Southern hospitality. Sometimes the house is even clean. People drink beverages and kids run around, until inevitably someone falls and skins a knee. Then the parents drink more to cope with the crying.

There was a time when thoughtful entertaining felt possible, before kids, chores, travel, and jobs blotted out every inch of free time on the calendar. The budgeted hours our parents had for cocktail parties and dinner fetes is a nebulous subscription that we can't quite figure out how to order.

Maybe my apprehension comes from my day job. I am a chef and restaurateur, the implication being that I kind of host an event every night. At home I yearn for a party that doesn't require a professional kitchen, fancy ice machines and a staff of fifty, and most of all I don't want to play restaurant. I want to hang out with friends and family and enjoy my time off. I want to make good food, but much simpler food than we make at the restaurants. This usually results in a quick, build-your-own kind of dinner (tacos!), with all of us hovering around a cluttered kitchen island, still covered in stacks of mail and bills and crumbs from breakfast and lunch. Our kids roll their eyes when the response to "What's for dinner?" is "Taco Night." (I'm sure our friends' kids do the same.) They like the food, but the event itself has developed into a bit of a rut. It's fun, but maybe we should show our guests a little more love.

I first met Annette in Athens at my house where she was styling a photo shoot for *Better Homes & Gardens*. The shoot was well planned and well thought out. She transformed our simple taco night into an event. Colorful napkins, crazy piñatas, and bright seasonal cocktails elevated our cherished but shopworn tradition. The party started with the setup, in which we all participated—arranging flowers, making paper pom poms with our daughters, layering fabrics on tables and counters, and, of course, cooking.

Annette orchestrated it with grace, ease, humor, and a touch of irreverence, making it possible for us to believe we could do it, too! She purchased, inexpensively, many of the supplies down the street at our neighborhood super mercado and supplied simple props, everyday objects dug out of cabinets or found in local flea markets. Our little kids easily executed Annette's craft ideas. Her linens, modestly repurposed by her own hand, looked lush and glamorous. It was a helluva shoot that never felt like work and quite the party.

With *Picture Perfect Parties*, Annette's gorgeous but attainable ideas and recipes are now available for keeps. We cannot wait to put it on our shelf (the cluttered one in the kitchen with our most-prized and most-used cookbooks). This comprehensive party planner provides blueprints to guide you—from DIY décor, to simple recipes (i.e., no marathon lists of ingredients), to choosing a playlist. Making our guests feel loved does not require a complicated event. Just a memorable one. Hide the bills and sweep the crumbs, let's plan this party.

introduction

MY STORY

I have always been a party girl. One of my earliest childhood memories is watching my glamorous Hungarian grandmother prepare lunch for our extended family of twenty in her kitchen at the back of her big apartment in Budapest. And so began my fascination with food, people, parties, preparations, and fun.

The most important lesson my grandmother taught me was to love all of your guests—make every guest feel special and make food that everyone will love to eat. Who knew that the secret to a great party could be so simple? But it's true: if you pay attention to these two things your parties will always be successful.

Every summer I watched her pour love upon her guests, treat everyone as if they were the most special person in the room, and effortlessly prepare delicious breakfasts, lunches, and dinners, always with great attention to the details. My grandmother was my first cooking instructor, but what she really taught me was how to be a host, and for that I am eternally grateful.

All her lessons and all those perfect parties led me to seek a career as a food stylist and a lifestyle expert. I started working with a commercial photographer twenty years ago as an assistant stylist, and I assisted a food stylist on the first day of my job. That day's work consisted of sorting through about 2,000 sandwich buns to find the perfect match for an Arby's advertising shoot. Not exactly the adventure and glamour of styling that I had dreamed of, but, nonetheless, my love affair with styling began on that day and I quickly absorbed all the knowledge I could glean.

Learning to organize my tasks on set so that photo shoots would flow smoothly was a huge lesson learned at the beginning of my career. My early years on a set gave me an eye for details and the organizational skills that serve me well to this day. To style a photograph, whether it's a plate of food or the furniture and décor in a room, I learned to see things as the camera saw them—as a composition. Every detail in a photograph is important, so perfection and attention to every detail is imperative.

Now I work with magazines and in television, on catalogs and on cookbooks, making entertaining lifestyle stories come to life. Whether I'm working on photo shoots, buying props, or producing a feature for a magazine, I have learned things that I use in my own family life. I've learned that whether I'm entertaining my family or a room full of friends, success is in the details—it's all about deciding on the perfect recipe and using the perfect setting.

Eventually, my obsession for making things beautiful in my work followed me home. With my family traditions of inviting, entertaining, and feeding people for breakfast, lunch, or dinner it was a natural step to apply my styling expertise to my own parties. With this book, I want to share with you what I have learned styling and hosting hundreds of dinner parties—my "tricks of the trade" for planning and setting the stage for a party, choosing the tastiest (and easiest) dishes to serve, and giving parties that are as fun and lovely for you as they are for your guests. I promise you this, on my grandmother's apron: You will become a great cook and a gracious host in no time.

Photos, from top: Grandmother Maria; three of my great aunts around a campfire with my aunt on the right; me and my son, Levi, and his friend, Jake.

The most important lesson my grandmother taught me was to love all of your guests—make every guest feel special and make food that everyone will love to eat. Who knew that the secret to a great party could be so simple?

ABOUT THIS BOOK

This is most definitely a cookbook for entertaining, in that it is filled with both delicious recipes and scores of ideas for creating the perfect tablescape. But it's not just a book of pretty tables (although I hope you think the table settings in this book are wonderful). It's not a book filled with glamorous or over-the-top expensive parties that are unachievable, either. The parties in this book will be, hopefully, inspiring and easy for you to accomplish. Most of the things you will need are probably already in your pantry, and nothing that I've suggested for do-it-yourself projects or plating are expensive to purchase. Think of it as a party primer, filled with tips and tricks from a seasoned stylist.

But I also think of it as a great cookbook disguised as a party book. Any of the recipes can be used anytime—not just for parties. It is my hope that I've given you a cookbook for every day and for every occasion.

HOW TO USE THIS BOOK

There are sixteen parties included in this book, starting with spring party ideas and continuing through the calendar of seasonal celebrations. Each party includes a menu and recipes, a list of all the elements you will need to create a beautiful table or dining environment, special do-it-yourself projects to make the party visually exciting, tips on styling and plating the food, and tons of photographs to help you create your own beautiful party.

I hope this will be a practical and useful guide you will refer to again and again. These parties are all about good taste and clever ideas—and not a big budget. You won't need super expensive dinnerware, crystal, silver, or monogrammed silk napkins to make any of these tables shine.

My motto is: Make it simple and make it gorgeous.

You will learn how to look at and use things that you already own—things from your pantry, on your shelves, and in your cupboards and closets—in a whole new way. I believe in organizing and repurposing your own things whenever possible. In addition, you will benefit from building your own "party toolbox" to give you the tools you need for any creative project in this book. You will learn to use the techniques I use as a photo stylist to make your cocktail and dinner parties, bridal showers, ladies' luncheons, family gatherings, and holiday celebrations smashing events.

Everyone has a creative instinct, and I have included lots of information to help you to tap into your own inner stylist, so that you, too, can give picture-perfect parties. I don't know about you, but I love it when guests compliment my food and my table. And I enjoy putting together a beautiful dinner party without the need for labor-intensive projects, or tons of expensive art supplies and endless pages of downloadable artwork.

The recipes are all time-tested favorites of mine—simple, delicious, and easy to make. Plus, each menu includes instructions to help you organize your preparation time so you are relaxed and ready for your guests to arrive.

If you love to entertain your friends and family, this book helps you show them how much you care by creating fantastic gatherings and priceless memories—as well as delicious food. Like my memories of summers with my grandmother, all the elements of your party will come to life.

BUILDING YOUR PARTY PANTRY

You will need some items to set your table, plate and present food, and set up a buffet. First off, don't buy anything until you organize what I call your "party pantry." Look at what you own and use the checklist below to collect trays, plates, glasses, and all the "props" of a pretty party. The things on this list are the basics you will need to create any party in this book.

Don't just search your kitchen cabinets for the things on this list; look in every room in your home—in your living room and den, and even your bedroom, foyer, garage, basement, or attic. I want you to shop your home for useable objects and items—think about repurposing and using things in a whole new way. Here's what you'll need to have:

3 baskets, wicker and/or metal

3 trays or flat objects that are food-safe and could be scrubbed and used to plate or gather food. I love old (or new) white enamelware. I find it online or at flea markets, and I have 1 rectangle, 1 square, and 1 round enamel tray.

12 glasses (mismatched is fine)

12 wine glasses, both red and white

12 champagne coupes

12 champagne flutes; these can be from a flea market, and mismatched.

2 wood trays or surfaces (like planking or old cutting boards): 1 rustic, 1 smooth

4 large ceramic or stone tiles; these can be used as platters for cheese or appetizers.

2 chalkboards or old signs, or anything you could use to write menus or messages for your guests.

Ribbon, string, yarn, twine, raffia, and ribbon

Wrapping paper: it makes great table runners, or use it to wrap vases or bottles.

Galvanized or enamel buckets: great for holding flowers, napkin rolls, breadsticks, or French bread. You will need 1 large, 1 medium, and 1 small bucket.

Vases and garden pots

Bottles and jelly or Mason jars: all sizes, at least 12 jars total (I like to save jam jars and run them through the dishwasher.)

Plates and platters: 1 small, 1 medium, and 1 large

Bowls: 3 small, 3 medium, and 3 large

Metal containers and wooden containers: 1 small, 1 medium, and 1 large of each

Wooden crates or small fruit crates/baskets from the grocery: 4 small and 4 medium-sized

3 yards of fabric, for table runners and tablecloths. (Old fabric is fine; even burlap from your garden shed can be washed, cut, and crafted into a table runner.)

Napkins and tablecloths: Old items can be overdyed, which is a great way to repurpose old and threadbare linens.

Mugs and tea cups (mismatched is fine)

Muffin tins and baking pans (I like vintage bakeware; the more beat up the better.)

12 each white dinner plates, salad plates

12 appetizer plates

10 espresso cups

10 coffee cups

12 white bowls, for soup, dessert, or salad

12 white dessert plates

12 knives, forks, spoons, dessert spoons, and dessert forks

3 small wooden servers, for jams and spreads

Mismatched flatware for serving meats and condiments

12 white and 12 natural linen napkins (If you do not already have linen napkins, these are the ones you should purchase. You will use them often.)

Linen tablecloths: 1 white and 1 dark (Like the linen napkins, good tablecloths are worth the investment and will stand up to years of use.)

Cocktail shaker

10 martini glasses

Novelty toothpicks

2 white cake stands: 1 small and 1 medium, plus 1 cake stand in a color, and 1 galvanized cake stand (optional)

Pie server

Ice cream scoop

8 placemats, for use only at a breakfast or lunch, or a very casual dinner

HOW TO STORE YOUR
PARTY PANTRY ESSENTIALS

Find a place in your home, garage, or basement to house your party pantry. You may need some storage shelves and a set of drawers. I suggest you shop flea markets or garage sales for a nice sturdy shelf unit if you don't already have some shelves in your home. Organizing everything makes it easy to pull essential party elements when you need them and it saves tons of time. As you will see, each of the parties in the book has a list of the essentials needed; if you already have them on hand when you want to throw a party, it's a real time saver!

Place everything in the lists above on the shelves and in drawers by category. That way, everything is contained in one place for easy access. For example: I like to store my linens in drawers by color. I store my serving forks, spoons, and all utensils by category, such as: carving knives, pie servers, mismatched flatware. Storing these items in drawers makes it effortless to find them when you need them. It also makes it easy to replenish or add new items to your party pantry.

BUILDING YOUR PARTY TOOLBOX

The items in your toolbox will be handy for any of the do-it-yourself projects in this book. Having these things on hand means no last-minute dashes to the store. You will use many of the same items in different ways throughout the book, so it's helpful to keep your toolbox stocked. See the Source Guide (page 222) for many of these items.

12 small jelly jars

White and natural parchment paper

Red and white baker's twine

Twine

12 glass votive candles

24 votive candles

Pinking shears

Plain packing labels, or decorative labels

Paper labels (the kind from an office supply store work great)

Floral wire

Wire nippers

Card stock in white and natural

Hot-glue gun

Scissors

Double-sided tape

Washi tape (decorative Japanese masking tape available at art stores or gift wrap stores), in different colors and patterns

Colorful duct tape

Adhesive letters and numbers (the decorative kind that come on sheets of vinyl or acetate, not the kind that go on your mailbox)

Tote bag, basket, or toolbox to organize these things

Decorative toothpicks

TIMING IS EVERYTHING

There is nothing worse than feeling rushed or unprepared for your party. Here are a few tips that will make prep time effortless. Additionally, time-saving tips are included within specific menus in the book to help organize your schedule.

STYLING SECRETS

Set the table and complete the DIYs one day before the party.

Arrange the flowers and complete the tablescape the night before.

Pull all the elements that you will need for the party, according to the "Elements" list at the end of each chapter.

Label platters, trays, and serving bowls with sticky notes, identifying the items to be placed in each of them.

Prep as much of the food as possible over a three-day span. Check recipes to decide which ones can be made in advance.

Review each of the recipes for cook time and make a list of which dishes should be made at the same time on the day of the party.

Balance your menu with regard to cooking methods—baking, grilling, and stovetop. You should have one of each preparation method on your menu so you are not slaving over a crowded cooktop when guests arrive. I suggest cooking just one stovetop recipe per menu on the day of the party. In other words, there should only be one dish that needs to be prepared and served hot from the cooktop.

elements of a party

The vessels, tableware, tools, and elements in this list are the essential ingredients I choose from to set a table and style each party. For the most part, they are things that you will find in your kitchen cabinets and around your home—things that become part of your party pantry. In each chapter, I will show you how to layer and combine them to create a beautiful and successful look for your party.

plates / *the perfect foundation*

jars
handblown +
handheld

mugs + cups
a warm cup of kindness

bowls

*simple comfort
in hand*

a woven wonderland

Baskets

glasses / *add a little sparkle*

paper
unroll, fit, fold & cut

cake stands
pretty pedestals all in a row

platters
delicious display

fabric /reams of texture

utensils
fork + function

ribbon + string

tie a bow or tie a knot

flowers

pretty petals + natural flourishes

trays

make it and contain it

wood

a slice of nature

The Parties

SPRING GARDEN PARTY

I plant a garden in the spring and fall and eat out of the garden year-round. The first signs of spring are cause for celebration, and even doubly so for any gardener. Working in and harvesting your own garden gives a great feeling of accomplishment. Guests are always thrilled when I tell them I'm serving something from my garden, such as the asparagus on this menu.

The use of burlap—a material I associate with gardening—to dress the table is a perfect complement to any floral arrangements that you use. Burlap says "gardening." You cover your garden with burlap in the spring to protect and insulate it from late cold. For this party, you will use burlap-covered lampshades, and layer a light-colored linen runner over a darker linen tablecloth. These layers add texture to your table and are an inexpensive way to achieve a rich look. I relate texture in décor and texture in food—I use both to cre-

ate an interesting menu and an interesting décor, so each is essential to these parties. Using cake stands of different heights in this décor adds another element of layering. Wood, burlap, linen, and fresh spring greens are all the color and texture that you need to make this party beautiful, bright, and fresh.

First, cover your table with a cloth, then add a table runner on top, and then start to construct a centerpiece by grouping cake stands of varying heights in the middle of the table. Place flower arrangements on top of each stand to create a quick and interesting centerpiece. Put all the platters, trays, and bowls on the buffet, and make your napkin roll-ups and place them on the table as well.

This party menu can also be used for a baby or wedding shower in the springtime.

menu

Olive Tapenade with Crostini

Baby Spring Salad
with Lemon-Shallot Vinaigrette

Grilled Asparagus with Mandarin Oil

Grilled Whole Rainbow Trout
with Mandarin Oil & Pistachios

Deconstructed Raspberry Cannoli

Add height and create a centerpiece for your buffet table using multiple cake stands of different colors and textures. I filled small vases with flowers from the garden to showcase the garden theme.

OLIVE TAPENADE
with Crostini
Serves 6

I used a wooden sculpture as the serving platter for this appetizer. It had been hanging on the wall of my guest room, and when I thought about how to serve this simple dish in an interesting way, it seemed a great answer to my problem. Find your own interesting serving plate to dress up any appetizer recipe.

OLIVE TAPENADE
1 cup pitted Kalamata olives
3 garlic cloves
3 tablespoons good-quality olive oil
1/4 teaspoon salt
1/2 teaspoon pepper
2 tablespoons fresh lemon juice
1/4 cup crumbled feta cheese

CROSTINI
1 French bread baguette
1/3 cup olive oil

For the tapenade: In a food processor, combine the olives, garlic, olive oil, salt, and pepper and pulse for 30 seconds. Add the lemon juice and pulse for an additional 30 seconds. Stir in the feta cheese.

For the crostini: Preheat the oven to 350° F.

Slice the baguette diagonally into 3/4-inch-thick slices and place in a single layer on a baking sheet. Brush each slice on both sides with the olive oil and bake for 5 minutes, or until golden brown.

Arrange the crostini on a platter along with a bowl or jar containing the olive tapenade.

Note: The olive tapenade may be made the day before the party and refrigerated in an airtight container until ready to serve. The crostini may be baked in the morning and stored in a large zip-top bag at room temperature until you are ready to serve.

BABY SPRING SALAD
with Lemon-Shallot Vinaigrette

Serves 6

This is an easy way to serve a salad, as it allows guests to mingle while eating and the glasses are easy to hold in one hand. Plate the salads individually in low, clear glasses and group them on the table. You will love how this presentation makes your table look fresh from the garden. Lemon and shallots in the dressing add a sprightly, tart accent to crunchy spring lettuce.

LEMON-SHALLOT VINAIGRETTE

1/2 cup olive oil

1/4 cup fresh lemon juice

1 shallot, finely diced

2 tablespoons chopped fresh thyme

1/2 teaspoon salt

1/2 teaspoon pepper

SALAD

4 small heads butter lettuce, torn into
   bite-size pieces (about 4 cups)

1/2 cup fresh baby peas

1 carrot, sliced into thin curls using a potato peeler

1 bunch baby radishes, trimmed and sliced
   into thin coins

For the vinaigrette: In a small mixing bowl, whisk together all the vinaigrette ingredients until well combined, and set aside.

For the salad: In each of 6 wide-mouth low drinking glasses, assemble each salad individually by layering first the lettuce and baby peas, then the carrot curls and radish coins. Drizzle each salad with 2 tablespoons of vinaigrette and serve.

Note: The Lemon-Shallot Vinaigrette can be made 3 days in advance, sealed in an airtight container, and refrigerated until the day of the party. Before the party, allow the dressing to sit at room temperature for 1 hour, then shake or whisk before using.

GRILLED ASPARAGUS
with Mandarin Oil

Serves 6

Tying these asparagus spears with food-safe twine or string is like offering your guests a gift. I love making pretty packages for my guests, and these little bundles of asparagus look great on a plate or a platter. Frame them by double-plating this dish, as I do. Mandarin orange olive oil is available online from O & Co. (see Source Guide, page 222).

2 bunches fresh asparagus

3 tablespoons olive oil

1/2 teaspoon salt

1/2 teaspoon pepper

4 tablespoons Mandarin orange olive oil

1 (10.75-ounce) can Mandarin oranges, drained

Preheat a grill to medium heat.

Trim the asparagus into 6-inch spears. Place the spears in a large bowl with the olive oil and toss to coat. Add the salt and pepper, and toss the spears again to coat evenly. Grill the asparagus for 8 to 10 minutes over a hot grill, turning every 2 minutes, until the spears are bright green but not charred. Remove the asparagus from the grill, drizzle with the Mandarin oil, and garnish the plate with Mandarin orange segments.

Note: You may grill the asparagus on the morning of the party. Place the grilled asparagus on a platter, cover loosely with plastic wrap, and keep at room temperature until you are ready to serve.

Styling Secrets

ASPARAGUS BUNCHES TIED WITH TWINE IS AN EASY SOLUTION TO MAKING A SIMPLE DISH LOOK SPECIAL—LIKE A GIFT FOR YOUR GUESTS!

SERVE YOUR SALAD COURSE IN A WAY THAT'S EASY TO HOLD AND EAT WHILE STANDING AND VISITING. USING A SMALL, WIDE-MOUTH GLASS MAKES A WONDERFUL PRESENTATION BECAUSE IT SHOWS OFF ALL THE BEAUTIFUL COLORS AND TEXTURES OF THE FRESH VEGETABLES.

USE THICK WOODEN DISKS AS RISERS TO ELEVATE DIFFERENT DISHES ON YOUR TABLE. IT ENHANCES THE VISUAL LOOK OF EACH DISH AND WILL GIVE YOUR BUFFET TABLE A LESS CLUTTERED APPEARANCE.

GRILLED WHOLE RAINBOW TROUT
with Mandarin Oil & Pistachios

Serves 6

You can usually find rainbow trout at high-end grocery stores, fish markets, and farmers' markets with a fish counter. I buy it at an Asian market that has a wide variety of fish at affordable prices, and well-trained fish butchers. Ask your fishmonger for whole rainbow trout, gutted, scales removed, with head, fins, and tails left on.

A square wooden serving tray has become a staple on my buffet table, providing a unique frame for fish or game dishes. Pick one of your own wooden trays to achieve this unusual presentation for your party.

½ cup roasted pistachios, shelled and
    coarsely chopped
1 (10.75-ounce) can Mandarin orange segments,
    with juice
Salt and pepper
3 (1- to 1¼-pound) whole rainbow trout,
    heads and tails on
3 tablespoons olive oil
1 lemon, sliced into thin rounds
½ cup (1 stick) butter
1 large shallot, peeled and finely chopped
2 teaspoons Mandarin orange olive oil (see p. 32),
    for drizzling
Italian parsley sprigs, for garnish

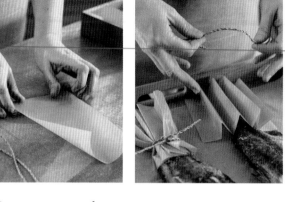

How to make
FISH TAILS

MATERIALS:

3 brown paper lunch bags
Food-safe kitchen twine, or raffia
Scissors

DIRECTIONS:

1. Cut the small paper bag horizontally across the top of bag, about 3 inches from the top, forming a long narrow band. Then cut the band to form one long strip and lay the paper band out flat on your tabletop.

2. Starting at one end of the band, fold the paper into ½-inch-wide pleats, folding forward then under to create pleats, and pressing the paper as you go to firm the folds.

3. Fan open the band and fit it around the fish tail to form a skirt.

4. Using rafia or twine, pinch and tie the top of the band to secure the skirt around the tail. You are ready to plate, garnish, and serve the fish.

Preheat a grill to medium-high.

In a food processer, combine the pistachios, 2 tablespoons of the Mandarin orange juice, and salt and pepper to taste. Pulse briefly for 10 seconds.

To prepare the trout, rinse the fish and pat dry with paper towels, then rub each fish on both sides with the olive oil. Sprinkle the fish on both sides with salt and pepper. Tuck 3 to 4 lemon slices within the cavity of each fish.

Place the trout on a sheet of lightly greased, heavy-duty aluminum foil and grill without turning for 8 to 10 minutes, or until the fish releases from the foil. Carefully turn the fish over and continue to cook for another 5 minutes, or until the fish flakes easily.

While the fish is grilling, sauté the shallots in the butter in a skillet over medium-high heat for 2 minutes. Stir in the pistachio mixture and Mandarin oranges with their remaining juice, and continue to cook for 5 minutes, or until the butter turns a light brown color.

Put "skirts" on each of the fish (see above) and arrange the fish on a serving tray. Pour some of the pistachio-orange butter over the trout, then drizzle with the Mandarin oil and garnish with parsley sprigs. Serve the remainder of the pistachio-orange butter on the side.

DECONSTRUCTED RASPBERRY CANNOLI

Makes 10

My favorite dessert when I'm in New York is a cannoli, preferably from an old Italian pastry shop in Little Italy. Since I am a big fan of the crunchy-sweet ricotta treat, I came up with this version for parties. (I never mind if there are leftovers!) You will love the process, since there is no messy piping of the filling into the shells. I buy my small cannoli shells from a local bakery. They are fresher and crispier than the packaged ones. The taste of fresh raspberries and raspberry sauce send this dessert's wow factor right over the top.

CHEESE FILLING

2 cups fresh ricotta cheese
2 ounces soft fresh goat cheese, at room
    temperature
1/4 cup confectioners' sugar
1/4 teaspoon ground cinnamon
2 teaspoons fresh lemon juice
1 cup baby chocolate chips

RASPBERRY SAUCE

1/4 cup sugar
3 pints fresh raspberries

TO SERVE

1 pint fresh raspberries
10 small cannoli shells, available at specialty
    stores, or substitute chocolate twirl cookies
Fresh basil leaves, for garnish

How to make NAPKIN FANS

MATERIALS:

6 square cotton table napkins
Twine
Scissors

DIRECTIONS:

1. Cut six 4-inch lengths of twine and set aside.

2. Fold a napkin into a small square: once in half, then repeat and fold in half again.

3. Starting at the side closest to you, make a 1-inch horizontal fold in the napkin, then fold the napkin under to make another fold of the same width. Repeat this until the napkin is completely folded. Press the folded napkin with your hands, so it retains the pleats. No ironing is necessary.

4. Tie a piece of twine around the center of the napkin. Fan the fabric out above and below the twine to form a fan.

For the filling: In a large mixing bowl, stir together the cheeses, confectioners' sugar, cinnamon, lemon juice, and chocolate chips and set aside.

For the sauce: In a large, heavy saucepan, combine the sugar and the 3 pints raspberries and cook over medium heat for 10 minutes, stirring occasionally. The raspberries will liquefy quickly, so be careful not to let them burn. Remove the saucepan from the heat and let the raspberries cool slightly.

Place a sieve over a large bowl and pour the cooled raspberry sauce through it to strain. Transfer the strained sauce to a plastic squeeze bottle fitted with a pointed cone top. Set aside until you are ready to assemble the dessert.

To assemble the desserts in individual glasses, spoon the cheese mixture to cover the bottom of each of 6 glasses, to a 3/4-inch depth. Next, squeeze a layer of raspberry sauce on top of the cheese, then repeat with another layer of the cheese mixture. Add a layer of fresh raspberries, another layer of cheese filling, and top each dessert off with more raspberry sauce.

If you are assembling these the morning of your party, you may cover each glass with plastic wrap and refrigerate until you are ready to serve.

When you are ready to finish and serve the dessert, remove the plastic wrap, stand a cannoli shell or a cookie up in the top of the dessert, and garnish each with a few small basil leaves.

SERVING PIECES
6 small appetizer plates
6 dinner plates

GLASS
10 juice glasses, for desserts
6 small clear glasses, for salads
6 wine glasses
1 cake stand

CERAMIC
3 vases, to hold forks
1 cake stand
2 vases for flowers

METAL
6 each: forks, knives, and spoons
1 cake stand
1 serving fork, for fish
1 tray, for dessert glasses

WOOD
1 wood riser (a slice of tree trunk works great)
1 pair of wooden tongs
2 wooden trays, for tapenade and trout dishes

TEXTILES
6 green napkins
1 natural linen tablecloth
1 linen table runner

PLATTERS + SERVING BOWLS
1 platter for asparagus
1 platter for trout

PAPER + STRING
Natural parchment paper
Natural twine
Paper cocktail napkins for wine glasses

DECOR
Natural preserved moss for around the salad,
in glasses, on the wooden disk
Hydrangeas, or flowers from your garden

AN
EASTER
LUNCH

FOR
FAMILY
& FRIENDS

MENU

Grilled Vegetable Bruschetta with Fresh Goat Cheese

Tuscan Sweet and Sour Kale

Potato Galette

Farro Salad with Olives and Pink Grapefruit

Roast Leg of Lamb Stuffed with Lemon and Herbs

Individual Fruit Trifles with Raspberry Sauce

Springtime brings special holidays and the start of warmer months. When my kids were little they loved the idea of the Easter bunny. Even though in our family Passover was the major spring religious holiday, I loved the idea of gathering their friends and ours and organizing an Easter egg hunt, so that they could enjoy the idea of an Easter bunny bringing eggs. What a wonderful childhood fantasy! Who can resist a sweet little bunny delivering sweet treats to children?

The idea for this party started when I saw a beautiful hand-painted pastel tablecloth in a market in the South of France. It was outrageously expensive and I thought, *I can make that*. I have had experience as a textile designer and painter, and I loved making eggs with the kids when they were little. Inspired by the sweet colors of Easter eggs, and wanting to achieve a hand-painted effect without spending a lot of money,

I created an easy project to paint a paper tablecloth. It's something the whole family can help with, it's inexpensive, and you can just ball it up and throw it away after your party.

This party works well as either an indoor or outdoor luncheon, although I would suggest doing the painting outdoors or in a covered area. That way, you won't sweat the drips and splashes!

If you are so inclined and your guests come casually dressed (in case of paint drips!), everyone can be invited to join in the decorating. Splattering paint on eggs and painting a tablecloth is a fun project for all ages. The time it takes to paint the paper and let it dry won't hold up your lunch, if you plan for guests to arrive early.

This party idea can be used for graduations and baby showers, too. Just use paint colors that are appropriate for your theme.

GRILLED VEGETABLE BRUSCHETTA with Fresh Goat Cheese

Makes 24

This tray of garlicky grilled vegetable bruschetta makes a colorful, edible centerpiece. Here's a great tip I learned about serving appetizers: If you want to get your guests to the table quickly, have your appetizer tray in the center of the table when they arrive. Make sure you grill the vegetables ahead of time, which makes assembly quick and easy.

½ red onion, peeled and quartered
¾ cup plus 2 tablespoons extra virgin olive oil
2 cloves garlic, peeled
1 teaspoon salt
¼ teaspoon pepper
1 small eggplant, sliced into ¾-inch rounds
1 medium zucchini, halved lengthwise
1 medium yellow squash, halved lengthwise
1 red bell pepper, left whole
4 Roma tomatoes, halved
1 lemon, halved and seeded
1 bunch asparagus, ends removed
1 loaf rustic bread
1 (10-ounce) log soft fresh goat cheese
Oregano sprigs, for garnish

Preheat a grill to medium-high heat.

Place the onion wedges in a square of aluminum foil and pour 2 tablespoons of the olive oil over the wedges, then seal the foil to make a loose package for grilling.

Pour the remaining ¾ cup olive oil into a large bowl. Use a Microplane grater over the bowl to grate the garlic into the oil, and add the salt and pepper.

Reserve ¼ cup of the garlic oil mixture for later use. Toss all the vegetables in the bowl with the remaining garlic oil mixture.

Place the onion packets on the grill and allow them to cook for 10 minutes. Add the eggplant, zucchini, squash, bell pepper, tomatoes, and lemon halves and grill for 5 minutes, then turn all the vegetables and continue to grill for 5 minutes, or until the bell pepper has a deep char and the vegetables show grill marks. As the other vegetables are cooking, check the packets of onions, and remove from the grill when the onion has caramelized. Add the asparagus spears during the last 3 minutes of grilling, and roll them so they grill evenly.

Run the red pepper under cold water until it is cool to the touch, then peel off the charred skin and remove the seeds from inside the pepper under running water. Place the pepper on paper towels to dry, then slice into ¼-inch ribbons and transfer to a platter. Cut the zucchini, squash, and eggplant into bite-sized pieces. Cut the asparagus spears into 1½-inch lengths.

Slice the bread into ¾-inch-thick slices and grill for 3 minutes on each side, or until the slices are toasted. You can also toast the bread slices in a 350° F oven for 5 minutes, then turn and toast for another 5 minutes. Place all the grilled veggies on a platter or sheet pan and drizzle the reserved garlic oil mixture over all. Then squeeze the grilled lemon over the vegetables.

Allow the vegetables to reach room temperature before you assemble the appetizers. Spread the goat cheese on the toasted bread slices and top each slice with a layer of grilled vegetables, in any combination. Garnish each with 1 fresh sprig of oregano. Note: These appetizers can be assembled a couple hours ahead, covered with plastic wrap, and allowed to sit at room temperature until ready to serve. The trick is to make sure that the vegetables are at room temperature when they are assembled.

Using a sheet of parchment paper inside the serving tray is an elegant touch, and a good choice if you are using an old, rustic, or wooden tray to display the food.

TUSCAN SWEET AND SOUR KALE

Serves 6 to 8

If you, your family, or friends don't like kale, you must try this recipe. It's a great vegetable and so good for you. I know you've probably heard that before, but if you try this dish, you'll be a convert! Even in our house, there aren't many dishes featuring kale that are everyone's favorite, but this is definitely one of them. The brown sugar and vinegar soften the bite of the milder "black" kale (also called Tuscan kale, lacinato kale, or cavolo nero); the combination of all three flavors is surprising and delicious.

12 large Tuscan kale leaves (10 cups)
3 tablespoons olive oil
2 garlic cloves, chopped
1/2 cup sliced yellow onion
2 tablespoons brown sugar
1/4 cup red wine vinegar
1/2 teaspoon salt
1/4 teaspoon pepper

Wash and dry the kale, cut the tough vein from the center of each leaf, then chop the leaves into 3-inch pieces.

In a large sauté pan over medium-high heat, heat the oil and sauté the garlic, onion, and brown sugar for 5 minutes, or until the oil is bubbly and brown. Add the vinegar, kale, salt, and pepper. Reduce the heat to medium, and continue to sauté for 10 minutes, or until the kale has wilted.

Remove from the heat and serve warm.

POTATO GALETTE

Serves 6 to 8

Here's a great way to serve this dish for a casual buffet or a family-style dinner: Allow the cooked galette to cool slightly, then cut it into wedges and carefully remove them from the skillet to a plate. Wash and dry the skillet and line it with enough parchment paper to reach up the sides of the pan, place the wedges back into the skillet, and sprinkle them with fresh thyme. It makes a lovely presentation without using a fancy platter or serving dish.

1/2 cup (1 stick) butter, melted
4 tablespoons chopped fresh thyme, divided
1 1/2 teaspoons sea salt
1/2 teaspoon pepper
3 pounds small Yukon gold potatoes, peeled

Preheat the oven to 425° F.

In a large cast-iron skillet, melt the butter and stir in 3 tablespoons of the chopped fresh thyme and the salt and pepper. Remove the butter mixture from the skillet and reserve in a bowl.

In a food processor fitted with the slicing blade, slice the potatoes into thin rounds and reserve in a bowl. Work quickly so the potatoes won't discolor.

Layer the sliced potatoes in the cast-iron skillet, and drizzle some of the melted butter mixture over each layer.

Place the skillet over medium heat for 5 minutes, or until the bottom layer of potatoes is lightly browned.

Transfer the skillet to the oven and cook for 1 hour, or until the top layer of potatoes has browned. Remove from the oven and allow the galette to cool slightly in the pan before cutting into wedges.

FARRO SALAD
with Olives and Pink Grapefruit

Serves 6 to 8

In my travels to Italy every summer I love to try new grains. One summer I bought some farro at the local store and it has become a staple in my pantries in Italy and in the US. This grain salad is something I made up one day in Italy using only things I had in my refrigerator and the pantry. Being miles from a grocery has occasionally called for some real creativity and led to a few wonderful discoveries! I adore farro and love to use it in salads. This has become a staple side dish on my menus. Feel free to add another grapefruit if you like more citrus. This salad is best made eight hours ahead to allow the flavors to mingle. In fact, it's best made the morning of the party; just cover it and leave it out at room temperature until you are ready to serve it.

Farro can be found in the grain aisle at most high-end grocery stores.

1 1/2 cups farro

1 1/2 teaspoons salt, divided

1 cup toasted walnuts

2 small bulbs fresh fennel, thinly sliced

1/2 cup chopped tender fennel tops

1 pink grapefruit, cut into segments

1/2 red onion, finely chopped

1 cup pitted niçoise olives, or your choice black olives

1 cup shaved Parmesan cheese (I use a potato peeler)

3 tablespoons balsamic vinegar

1/4 cup extra virgin olive oil

1/2 teaspoon pepper

Preheat the oven to 350° F.

Bring the farro to a boil in a pot with 4 cups water and 1/2 teaspoon of the salt, then reduce the heat and allow the farro to simmer for 30 minutes, or until tender. The farro will absorb all the liquid. Set aside to cool.

While the farro is cooling, spread the walnuts on a baking sheet or in a pie pan and toast in the oven for 5 minutes, or until they are lightly browned.

In a large mixing bowl, toss together the cooled farro, the fennel, fennel tops, grapefruit, chopped red onion, 1/2 cup of the toasted walnuts, the olives, and the shaved Parmesan, along with the balsamic vinegar, olive oil, remaining 1 teaspoon salt, and the pepper. When you are ready to serve, garnish the salad with the remaining toasted walnuts.

ROAST LEG OF LAMB
Stuffed with Lemon and Herbs

Serves 6 to 8

If you love lemons, you will love them in this dish. Meyer lemons, which are smaller, sweeter, and softer than Eureka (or true) lemons, would be wonderful in this if they are available. If you use regular lemons, I suggest you halve the lemon wedges so they are smaller.

MARINADE
1/4 cup olive oil

1 teaspoon salt

1/2 teaspoon black pepper

3 tablespoons grated lemon zest (from about 5 small lemons)

2 tablespoons fresh lemon juice

3 cloves garlic, minced

2 tablespoons chopped fresh rosemary

2 tablespoons honey

1 teaspoon Dijon mustard

1 (4-pound) boneless leg of lamb

LEMON AND HERB STUFFING
1/2 cup raisins

1 teaspoon sea salt, divided

2 small lemons, cut into small wedges

3 tablespoons olive oil

3 tablespoons butter

1/4 cup chopped shallots

1 cup panko breadcrumbs

1/2 cup chopped pitted green olives

3 tablespoons chopped fresh Italian parsley

2 tablespoons fresh thyme leaves

1/2 cup chicken stock

For the marinade: Combine all the marinade ingredients in a small mixing bowl and set aside.

For the lamb: Remove its netting and place the leg of lamb in a large zip-top plastic bag. Pour the marinade over the lamb in the bag and seal the bag. Massage the marinade so that it covers the lamb, and refrigerate for at least 3 hours. You can also do this step a day ahead and leave the lamb in the fridge overnight.

For the stuffing: In a small bowl, toss the raisins with 1/2 teaspoon of the sea salt. In a separate small bowl, toss the lemon wedges with the remaining 1/2 teaspoon sea salt.

Heat the oil and butter in a large saucepan over medium heat. Add the shallots and sauté for 3 to 4 minutes, until lightly browned. Add the raisins, lemons, breadcrumbs, olives, parsley, thyme, and chicken stock to the saucepan and sauté for 5 minutes. Remove from the heat and set aside.

Preheat the oven to 425° F.

Place the marinated leg of lamb fat-side down on a cutting board lined with butcher or parchment paper and pound it with a mallet until it is flat and an even thickness.

Mound the stuffing in a line down the middle of the lamb, then wrap the sides of the lamb around the stuffing, tuck in the ends, and tie the lamb with kitchen twine to secure the stuffing. Rub the lamb with salt and pepper and place it on a rack in a roasting pan fat-side up. Roast for 15 minutes, then reduce the heat to 325° F and continue to roast for 30 to 45 minutes, or until it reaches your desired degree of doneness. Test for doneness with a meat thermometer placed into the middle of the leg of lamb. For medium-rare, the thermometer should read 130° to 135° F; for medium it should be 140° to 145° F; and for well done it should read 150° to 160° F. When the lamb is cooked to your desired temperature, remove it from the oven and let it rest for 15 minutes. Remove the string before carving.

Styling Secrets

FOR THE BRUSCHETTA, USE AN UN-EXPECTED SERVING VESSEL, LIKE THIS METAL CARRIER.

THE FARRO SALAD LOOKS GREAT IN A SUPER-ELONGATED OVAL BOWL.

TO SERVE THE POTATO GALETTE, USE THE SAME SKILLET IN WHICH THE DISH WAS COOKED AND LINE IT WITH PARCHMENT PAPER.

How to make DESSERT NESTS

These nests should be made at least a day before your party, or even earlier if you prefer.

MATERIALS:

6 birds' nests, from a
  craft store
1 can white spray paint
6 stemmed dessert glasses
2 yards hot pink yarn
Painter's tarp or dispos-
  able paper (newspaper
  works great)
Scissors

DIRECTIONS:

1. Arrange the nests on a work surface covered with a tarp and spray them all over with white paint. You will need to apply two coats of spray paint. Allow them to dry overnight.

2. When the nests have dried, use your scissors to cut a slit halfway into the nest, from the outside to the center. Do not cut the nests in half.

3. Gently open the slit enough to wrap the nest around the stem of a dessert glass.

4. Tie a length of yarn around the nest to secure it to the stem of the dessert glass. Now the glasses are ready for you to assemble the dessert in them.

INDIVIDUAL FRUIT TRIFLES
with Raspberry Sauce

Makes 6 to 8

This rates as the easiest "wow factor" dessert ever. The easy do-it-yourself nest wrap for the stemmed glasses will delight guests and create a picture-perfect finish to the meal. Plus, you can make these desserts ahead and stash them in the refrigerator until you are ready to serve. The cake will soak up the sauce—that's the "trifle" part of the dessert.

RASPBERRY SAUCE

1 pint raspberries
1/2 cup sugar

FRUIT TRIFLE

1 angel food cake, store-bought
1 pint strawberries, hulled and sliced
2 pints raspberries
1 pint blueberries
1 quart whipping cream
1/2 cup sugar

For the sauce: In a medium saucepan over medium-high heat, stir together the raspberries and sugar and cook for 10 minutes, or until the raspberries have reduced to a sauce, then remove from the heat and set aside to cool. When the raspberry sauce is cooled, strain it through a fine sieve fitted over a bowl.

For the trifles: Cut the cake into 1-inch cubes. In a large bowl, toss together the strawberries, raspberries, and blueberries. In the bowl of a mixer, combine the cream and sugar and whip on high for 3 to 5 minutes, until soft peaks form. Set aside.

To assemble the individual trifles, put 2 cubes of cake in the bottom of each of 6 champagne coupes, then add a layer of berries on top of the cake, then a layer of the sauce, and a layer of the whipped cream. Repeat the layering until each coupe is filled to the top. Refrigerate the individual trifles until ready to serve.

How to make
PAINTED LINENS

MATERIALS:

6 to 8 white cotton napkins
3 colors of neon fabric paint, your choice
   of colors, available at craft or art stores
3 disposable plastic cups, to hold paint
3 (1- to 2-inch width) paintbrushes
Painter's tarp or disposable paper
   (newspaper works great) to protect the
   painting area
Laundry drying rack
Iron
Ironing board

DIRECTIONS:

1. Place 2 tablespoons of each paint color
in a separate disposable plastic cup and
stir 1 tablespoon of water into each cup.
The paint should have a runny consistency.

2. Lay the napkins out flat on a work surface lined with a tarp or paper.

3. Paint with broad strokes on a napkin,
working quickly. Wash the brush each time
you are ready to apply another color. Colors
can run and blend together, so if you don't
want a blended effect, let the fabric color
dry before applying another color.
Splattering is achieved by holding the paint-
soaked brush vertically, brush up, about 1 foot
above the fabric, and flicking the paint onto
the fabric with a quick snap of your wrist.

4. Lay flat or hang the napkins on a drying rack and allow them to dry overnight.

5. The next day, you are ready to wash,
press, and fold the paint-splattered napkins.

How to make a
SPLATTER-PAINT CENTERPIECE

This is a painterly alternative to dying eggs for Easter. These objects can be grouped in the center of the table to form a delightful centerpiece. The ceramic pieces should be white or a pale pastel color, for contrast with the splatter paint. Try to find eggs at the store packaged in a pastel carton that will fit the color scheme.

MATERIALS:

3 colors of neon acrylic paint, your
   choice of colors, available at craft
   or art stores
Painter's tarp or disposable paper
   (newspaper works great) to protect
   the painting area
3 disposable plastic cups, to hold
   paint
4 egg cups
1 ceramic egg carton (this one is
   from Anthropologie)
12 hard-boiled eggs, in the carton
   (the eggs won't be eaten, but it's
   easier to use with hard-boiled eggs)
3 interesting white dessert plates
3 paintbrushes

DIRECTIONS:

1. Place 2 tablespoons of each paint
color in a separate disposable plastic
cup and stir 1 tablespoon of water into
each cup. The paint should have a runny
consistency.

2. Set the open carton of hard-boiled
eggs, the plates, and the egg cups on a
work surface covered with a painter's
tarp or disposable paper, leaving enough
room around each object to allow the
paint to reach all sides.

3. Dip the brushes into the paint and
flick the paint at the eggs, plates, and
holders, splattering as much or as little
paint on them as you like.

4. Allow the objects to remain on the
tarp to dry for 1 hour, then arrange them
on the table as a centerpiece.

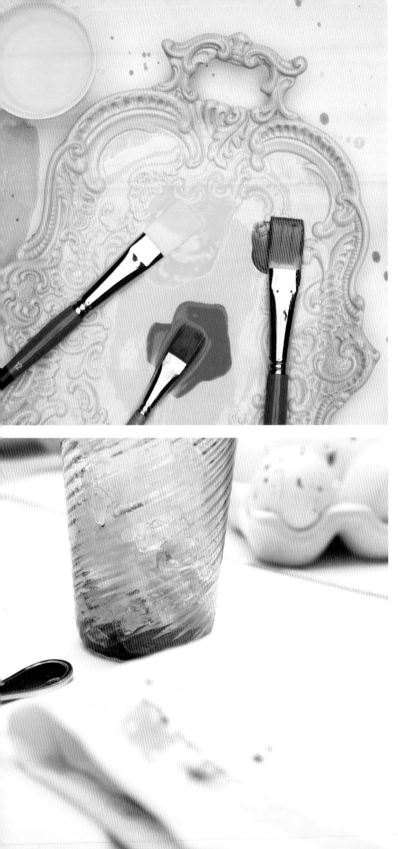

When using a very busy idea like splattering paint, try to stick to all-white plates and vessels. Mixing and matching several shades of white is fine. This will keep the theme less busy and more focused. If you use an occasional colored vessel, match it to one of your paint colors.

How to make a

HAND-PAINTED TABLECLOTH

The paintbrushes and plastic cups are repeated in this list, so you can use these same materials for both painting projects; however, you will need a different type of paint.

MATERIALS:

1 (50-inch-wide) roll white craft paper
3 colors of neon acrylic paint (your choice of colors), available at craft or art stores
3 disposable plastic cups, to hold paint
3 paintbrushes

DIRECTIONS:

1. Roll the white craft paper out on your dining table and cut to fit, allowing at least 3 inches overhang on all four sides of the table.

2. Start at the narrower end and fold the paper tablecloth in half vertically, then fold in half again, and again into thirds, then use your hands to press creases in the paper.

3. Place 2 tablespoons of each paint color in a separate disposable plastic cup and stir 1 tablespoon of water into each cup. The paint should have a runny consistency.

4. Unfold the creased paper and place it on the dining table creased sides up. Paint the creased folds using the different colors and creating color lines across the paper. You may let the colors blend and run together if you like. Otherwise, paint one color and wait for it to dry before you paint the next.

5. Use the brushes to splatter paint all over the paper tablecloth. Splattering is achieved by holding the paint-soaked brush vertically, brush up, about 1 foot above the paper, and flicking the paint onto the paper with a quick snap of your wrist.

6. Let the painted paper tablecloth dry for 30 minutes, or as long as it takes for the paint to feel dry to the touch. Cover your paint cups with plastic wrap while the tablecloth is drying, so that the paint will be ready for the next project—painting the platters and the eggs.

7. Next, lay the dry paper out on your dinner table and crease the paper along the edges of the table so that it will stay in place. You may also choose to turn the edges of the paper under the table and tape the paper tablecloth in place underneath.

8. Set the table using only your plates and positioning them around the table where guests will be seated.

9. Paint a circle around the plates using the plate as a guide. You may choose to paint a circle with one color, then use another brush to paint a freeform circle in another color around the first. For my tablecloth, I chose hot pink and acid green. Remove the plates and splatter paint on the paper at this point if you like. Allow the tablecloth to dry completely again before you set the table with dinnerware and utensils.

SERVING PIECES
6 white dinner plates
1 platter, for the lamb
1 medium bowl, for the kale
1 low-sided bowl, for the farro salad
1 plate or skillet, for the potato galette
4 ceramic egg cups
1 ceramic egg carton

GLASS
6 colorful water glasses
6 wine glasses
6 short-stemmed glasses,
for the trifles

METAL
6 each forks, knives, spoons
6 small spoons, for dessert
1 carrier, or basket, for appetizers
1 carving knife and serving fork,
for lamb
3 serving spoons, for farro
salad, kale, and galette

TEXTILES
White napkins
White paper tablecloth

PAPER + STRING + YARN
1 (50-inch) roll white craft paper,
for the painted tablecloth
Hot pink yarn
White parchment paper, to line
appetizer carrier and
galette skillet

CINCO DE MAYO

PARTY

Cinco de Mayo, the fifth of May, falls close to our wedding anniversary, so I love to throw a little south-of-the border celebration. Everyone loves Mexican flavors, and this food is perfect for an outdoor buffet, so this is a party we look forward to every year.

Even if you've never been to Mexico, you'll recognize the use of bright colors and patterns from that country. Cutout tissue-paper banners are traditional Mexican party décor, and add to the lively use of color, fabric, and patterns.

For this party, I try to keep the décor as texturally interesting as the menu. Textures are as important to the look of your party as they are to the taste of the food. For a buffet table, I lug my kitchen table outside because it's wood and has a rustic look. Wooden servers and hand-hammered metal trays enhance the tablescape, and the combination of rough, shiny, and smooth objects on the table adds to the visual excitement. Bright pops of colorful paper starbursts and die-cut flags hang above the table and flutter in the May breeze. Don't be afraid to use plenty of little candles and those big glass Mexican votive candles with religious icons on them. I get them at the grocery store here in Atlanta. If you have a Mexican market in your town, shop there for simple ideas to add to the table. Make sure to have a lively music playlist and plenty of guacamole and tortilla chips on hand.

Perhaps the most complicated DIY project in this book—overdying fabrics to create bright new patterns—is in this chapter, but it is so worth doing. Using old or vintage fabrics to create beautiful new table linens will lay the decorative groundwork for this colorful Mexican feast—plus, you will have beautiful linens you can use again and again.

Chilled Gazpacho

Guacamole

Salsa Verde

Grilled Pineapple
with Coconut Sour Cream Drizzle

Coca-Cola Ancho Chile
Pulled Brisket Soft Tacos

Slow-Cooked Black Beans
with Lime and Crispy Onions

Homemade Cinnamon
Ice Cream Sundae
with Sweet Tortilla Chips

CHILLED GAZPACHO

Serves 6 to 8

Serving chilled soup made from fresh ingredients during warm months is a healthy addition to any menu. I once prepared this soup for a small professional gathering at my home and every single person asked me for the recipe; in my book, that makes this one a winner. The key to the recipe is cutting all the vegetables to the same uniform size. I like to use ordinary water goblets for individual servings. Place spoons in each glass or alongside the glasses for easy serving. Begin making this a day before you plan to serve it because the flavors need time to marry.

SOUP

1/2 cup red wine vinegar

1/2 cup olive oil

3 cups baby grape tomatoes, quartered

2 garlic cloves, minced

6 cups fresh tomato juice or 1 (64-ounce)
    bottle tomato juice

1 cup salsa, your favorite brand and heat

1 large red bell pepper, seeded and cut into
    1/2-inch dice

1/2 medium red onion, cut into 1/2-inch dice

1 medium cucumber, cut into 1/2-inch dice

1 medium yellow squash, cut into 1/2-inch dice

1 medium zucchini, cut into 1/2-inch dice

2 carrots, peeled and cut into 1/2-inch dice

3 celery ribs, cut into 1/2-inch dice

3 pickled jalapeños, finely chopped

1 small bunch fresh cilantro, stemmed and
    chopped

1/2 teaspoon salt

1/2 teaspoon pepper

CROUTONS

1 loaf French bread, cut into 10 (1-inch-thick) slices

3 tablespoons olive oil

1 cup Greek-style plain yogurt

For the soup: Combine all the ingredients in a large bowl and mix well. Cover with plastic wrap and refrigerate overnight.

For the croutons: The next day, preheat the oven to 375° F.

Lightly brush the bread slices on both sides with the olive oil. Place the bread slices on a baking sheet, and bake for 10 minutes, or until the bread is golden brown.

To assemble the gazpacho, place a slice of toasted bread in the bottom of each glass, ladle the chilled soup on top of the crouton, and serve with a dollop of the Greek-style plain yogurt on top.

GUACAMOLE

Serves 6 to 8

The lime juice will keep the avocados from oxidizing for a few hours, but it's best to make this just before guests arrive. I like to serve guacamole in a free-form pottery bowl. Spread a large linen napkin atop a cutting board, place the bowl of guacamole on the napkin, and spread tortillas chips generously on the napkin around the bowl. Guests will go for the "chips and dip" throughout the party, so place the serving board at a spot on the table that you can easily get to when it's time to replenish these items during the party. I use store-bought tortilla chips because of the wide variety that are available in most supermarkets.

4 ripe avocados, halved and pitted
3 tablespoons fresh lime juice
1/2 cup chopped tomato
2 garlic cloves, minced
1/3 red onion, finely diced
1/2 cup chopped fresh cilantro
1/4 teaspoon sea salt
5 drops Cholula hot sauce, or your favorite brand

Scoop the avocado into a bowl, and smash with a fork. Add the remaining ingredients and stir to combine.

SALSA VERDE

Makes 3 cups

This is a make-ahead recipe that tastes better if refrigerated 24 hours before using. Salsa verde means "green sauce," and the tomatillos give a tart flavor to this wonderful sauce.

12 to 15 tomatillos, husked
3 canned chiles, El Paso brand or your favorite
1 yellow onion, peeled and halved
1 teaspoon salt
5 garlic cloves, minced (I use a Microplane grater for this)
3 tablespoons olive oil
1 cup chopped fresh cilantro
2 tablespoons fresh lime juice
1 fresh jalapeño, finely diced (optional)

Preheat the oven to 350° F.

In a large bowl, toss the tomatillos, chiles, onion, salt, and garlic with the olive oil to coat. Transfer the ingredients to a baking sheet and bake for 20 minutes.

Allow the roasted vegetables to cool to room temperature on the baking sheet, then transfer them to the bowl of a food processor fitted with a chopping blade. Add the cilantro, lime juice, and fresh jalapeño (if using) and pulse for 5 seconds.

Pour the salsa verde into a container fitted with a lid, or cover tightly with plastic wrap and refrigerate for 24 hours before serving, to allow the flavors to marry. Serve with chips and quacamole.

GRILLED PINEAPPLE

with Coconut Sour Cream Drizzle

Serves 6 to 8

If you have never grilled fruit, you may not know that it is a fantastic way to eat seasonal fruit. The sweetness of the grilled pineapple adds the perfect balance to the spicy brisket and salsas, and can be a great accompaniment to grilled fish, too.

2 large pineapples, peeled, cored, and sliced
   into 3/4-inch rings
2 tablespoons olive oil
1/4 teaspoon sea salt
1 cup sour cream
1 tablespoon fresh lime juice
1/4 cup sweetened shredded coconut
2 fresh red chiles, thinly sliced,
   or 1/2 teaspoon crushed red pepper flakes

Preheat a grill to medium heat.

In a large bowl, toss the pineapple slices with the oil and sea salt. Place the pineapple rings directly on the grill and cook for 2 to 3 minutes, then turn gently and cook for another 2 to 3 minutes, or until grill marks appear. Arrange the grilled pineapple on a serving platter.

Preheat the oven to 325° F and toast the coconut in a small pan for 3 minutes, or until it is golden brown.

In a plastic squeeze bottle, combine the sour cream and lime juice and shake to mix well. Drizzle the sour cream–lime sauce over the grilled pineapple rings, and sprinkle them with the toasted coconut and chiles.

Styling Secrets

A MASS OF SPOONS DISPLAYED IN A LARGE WATER GLASS IS A VERY FUNCTIONAL PRESENTATION AND IS PERFECT FOR THIS CASUAL PARTY.

SERVING THE GAZPACHO IN STEMMED WATER GLASSES IS A FUN WAY TO PRESENT THE SOUP. PLACE TINY SPOONS INTO EACH GLASS, FOR GUESTS TO PICK UP.

USING COLORFUL VOTIVE CANDLES STREWN ALL AROUND THE TABLE, WITH COLORFUL BOWLS TO HOLD THE CANDLES, CREATES A FIESTA AMBIENCE.

COCA-COLA ANCHO CHILE PULLED BRISKET SOFT TACOS

Serves 6 to 8

Because I live in Atlanta, Coca-Cola just seemed a natural ingredient to include in this brisket recipe. Proud Atlantans seem to find ways to include Coke in dozens of recipes. I have been developing this one for years. With the addition of ancho chile powder, I knew I had created something special. This brisket, shredded and stuffed into a tortilla with all the trimmings, will make your Cinco de Mayo a spicy celebration indeed.

BRISKET AND BRAISING SAUCE

1 (5- to 6-pound) beef brisket, trimmed of fat (I like to leave a little fat)
1 tablespoon sea salt, divided
1 teaspoon pepper, plus 1 teaspoon for rubbing on the brisket
1/4 cup olive oil
1 (28-ounce) can crushed tomatoes, with their juices
1 cup ketchup
2 (12-ounce) cans Coca-Cola
1 medium red onion, sliced
1/2 cup (packed) brown sugar
1/4 cup ancho chile powder
1/4 cup chili powder
10 cloves garlic, minced
3/4 cup red wine vinegar

TO SERVE

16 flour or corn tortillas
1 cup chopped onion (about 1 medium onion)
1 cup thinly sliced radishes
1 cup chopped fresh cilantro
2 cups crumbled queso fresco cheese
1/2 cup sliced fresh jalapeños
4 limes, cut into wedges

Create a self-serve taco station. Put the brisket in a tray and set it on a wooden cutting board along with several mismatched forks to use for serving. Arrange the warm tacos on the wooden cutting board next to the brisket.

Preheat the oven to 350° F.

Rub the brisket all over with 1 teaspoon of the salt and the pepper. Heat the olive oil in a large skillet over high heat and sear all sides of the brisket until browned, about 5 minutes per side.

In a large mixing bowl, stir together all the remaining sauce ingredients and season with the remaining 2 teaspoons salt and pepper to taste. Pour the braising sauce into a large roasting pan, then carefully add the seared brisket to the pan. Cover the pan with aluminum foil and tightly seal it around the edges. Bake the brisket in the preheated oven for 20 minutes, then reduce the heat to 300° F and continue to bake for 6 to 7 hours, until fork tender.

Remove the roasting pan from the oven, remove the foil, and allow the brisket to rest in the pan at room temperature for 1 hour.

Using 2 large forks, shred (or "pull") the brisket apart. Reserve 2 cups of the sauce from the pan and transfer it to a large mixing or serving bowl. Toss the pulled brisket in the sauce before serving, or serve the sauce on the side.

When you are ready to serve, wrap the soft tortillas in aluminum foil and warm them for 10 minutes in an oven preheated to 200° F. Serve the brisket alongside the warm tortillas and bowls of the assorted toppings.

SLOW-COOKED BLACK BEANS with Lime and Crispy Onions

Serves 6 to 8

Southerners love beans and so do I. I start cooking them the morning of the party and let them cook all day. The crispy onions in this recipe are a sophisticated twist on the traditional way of serving black beans with chopped onions. Textural contrast is really important to me when I'm putting a dish together, so I try to add a little crunch when I can. I use these crispy onions on other dishes, too, such as baked potatoes and grilled steaks. Try them on your favorite dishes to add additional flavor and crunch.

2 cups dried black beans
3 garlic cloves, crushed
2 teaspoons sea salt
2 to 3 tablespoons fresh lime juice

CRISPY ONIONS
1 large sweet onion, thinly sliced
1 1/2 cups all-purpose flour
1 1/2 cups canola oil
1 teaspoon sea salt

Rinse and soak the beans in 3 quarts water overnight. When you are ready to cook, drain and rinse the beans.

Bring the beans, 5 cups water, and the garlic to a boil in a heavy large saucepan over high heat, then reduce the heat to low and simmer, uncovered, for 4 to 5 hours.

After 2 hours, stir in the sea salt. Add extra water as needed. (The beans should be tender with a creamy consistency when done.) Stir the lime juice into the cooked beans before serving.

For the onions: About 1 hour before the party, toss the onions in a bowl with the flour, then shake off the excess flour. In a large skillet, heat the oil over high heat. Add the onion slices in 2 or 3 batches, and fry, tossing in the oil to ensure they don't stick together, for 5 to 7 minutes, or until they are crispy and golden brown. Remove the onions using a slotted spatula and drain on paper towels.

How to make
SILVER LUMINARIES
and Cactus Bags

Makes 3 bags with candles,
3 with cacti

MATERIALS:

6 (5 1/8 x 3 1/8-inch) Kraft paper
  lunch bags
1 can silver spray paint
5 pounds decorative sand, found
  at a craft store or garden center
3 votive candles
3 small cactus plants, potted
  (plastic pots are fine)
Painter's tarp or disposable paper
  (newspaper works great)

DIRECTIONS:

1. Lay the paper bags flat on a work surface covered with the tarp and spray one side of the bags with the silver paint. Allow the paint to dry. Note: the sides of the bags will remain unpainted.

2. When the first side is dry, turn the bags over and paint the other side. Allow that side to dry.

3. Open 3 of the bags and fold the top of each bag down twice so that it forms a 2-inch cuff.

4. Fill the 3 bags with sand halfway full and place a votive candle securely in the sand in each bag.

5. To make the cactus bags, use the remaining 3 folded bags and follow the directions in Step 3. Place a small potted cactus in the bottom of each bag. Pour sand over the top of the cactus pot until it reaches the top of the pot. Add enough sand around the base of the cactus to conceal the pot.

Sprinkle with the sea salt before serving.

Spoon the onions on top of the beans, or serve them in a bowl alongside the beans for guests to serve themselves.

HOMEMADE CINNAMON ICE CREAM SUNDAE

with Sweet Tortilla Chips

Serves 6 to 8

CINNAMON ICE CREAM

1 1/2 cups whole milk

1 cup heavy cream

1 cup sugar

2 large eggs, beaten, plus 1 large egg yolk

2 teaspoons ground cinnamon

1 teaspoon sea salt

1 whole vanilla bean, halved lengthwise, seeds
   scraped and reserved

SWEET TORTILLA CHIPS

1 cup canola oil

1 package small soft flour tortillas, cut in half

1 cup confectioners' sugar

1 jar caramel ice cream topping, your favorite
   brand

For the ice cream: In a medium saucepan over low heat, whisk together the milk, cream, and sugar. Continue to whisk over low heat until the milk begins to bubble. Remove from the heat.

In a small bowl, whisk together the eggs and yolk. Stir 1 cup of the mixture into the beaten eggs until combined. Pour the egg mixture back into the saucepan and cook over low heat, stirring, until the mixture is thick enough to coat the back of a spoon. Set aside to cool.

When the mixture has cooled, add the cinnamon, salt, and reserved vanilla bean seeds and whisk to blend. Add the vanilla bean pods to the pan and refrigerate, covered, until very cold, at least 1 hour.

Remove the vanilla pods. Transfer the custard to the ice cream maker and process according to the manufacturer's instructions.

When the ice cream is made, transfer it to a loaf pan lined with plastic wrap and freeze until ready to serve.

To prep the dessert ahead of time, scoop servings of ice cream into the cups early in the day and place the cups in the freezer until you are ready to serve.

For the tortilla chips: Heat the oil over high heat in a heavy cast-iron pot, and fry the soft tortillas for 2 minutes until golden. Remove and drain on paper towels. When you are ready to serve, sprinkle the tortillas liberally with confectioners' sugar. Spoon the individual servings of ice cream into Mason jars, and drizzle with the caramel topping, then place a tortilla chip on top of each scoop of ice cream.

Styling Secrets

SCATTER SILVER-PAINTED PAPER BAGS FILLED WITH SAND VOTIVES AND CACTI AROUND THE TABLE FOR A SOUTHWESTERN LOOK.

ICE CREAM SUNDAES SERVED IN PAPER CUPS ARE EASY TO PLATE. PLACE THE SUNDAES ON A MEXICAN-STYLE OR OTHER COLORFUL TRAY TO MATCH THE FESTIVE THEME OF THE PARTY.

USING WOODEN ICE CREAM SPOONS TO EAT THE INDIVIDUAL CUPS OF ICE CREAM IS A FUN AND RETRO TOUCH.

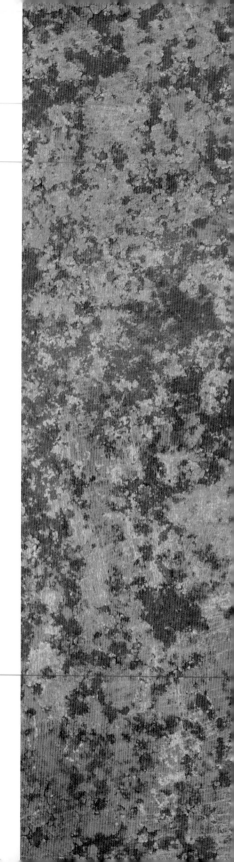

How to make
OVERDYED VINTAGE LINENS

MATERIALS:

1 fiber-reactive dye kit (see Source Guide, page 222; the kit will contain all the ingredients called for in the directions below, including the soap, dye, urea, and soda ash)

Rubber gloves

1 medium mixing bowl

2 (1-gallon) buckets

Iron

Ironing board

3 to 4 yards of fabric

DIRECTIONS:

1. Wash the fabric to be dyed with the soap provided by the dye manufacturer (in the dye kit), then dry the fabric.

2. In a medium mixing bowl, prepare the liquid concentrate: Mix together 1 cup water, 2 to 4 tablespoons urea, and 2 tablespoons dye.

3. In a bucket, prepare a soda solution by stirring 9 tablespoons soda ash into 1 gallon warm water.

4. Put on rubber gloves to handle the liquid concentrate during the dying process.

5. Place the fabric in a separate empty bucket and pour the liquid concentrate on top, pressing the fabric with your gloved hands so that the liquid completely covers the fabric. Press out any air bubbles, and let the fabric sit for 15 minutes in the concentrate.

6. Next, add the soda solution, and press the fabric again to completely cover with the liquid.

7. Leave the fabric to soak in the dye mixture for 1 hour, then, wearing rubber gloves, remove and wring out in running water. Rinse the fabric until the water runs clear.

8. Wash the dyed fabric in hot water in your washer, then dry in the dryer.

9. Press with a hot iron.

SERVING PIECES
10 dinner plates
10 water goblets, for gazpacho

GLASS
1 water glass, to hold spoons
8 small glasses, for individual salsas
5 brightly colored glasses for the votive candles

METAL
10 each soupspoons, forks, and knives
Metal tray, for brisket
3 forks, for serving brisket
10 small spoons, for individual salsas
Metal bowl, for black beans
1 serving spoon
Silver tray, for grilled pineapple
1 small serving fork
Metal lanterns
Large tub for beverages

TEXTILES
10 brightly colored napkins
1 large brightly colored napkin,
for tortilla chips

CERAMIC
Pottery bowl, for cloth napkins
Pottery, or rustic bowl, for guacamole

WOOD
Wooden cutting board, for brisket tray
Brightly colored tray, for guacamole
Wooden serving spoon, for guacamole
Disposable spoons, for ice cream

PLASTIC
Squeeze bottle, for sour cream–lime sauce
with pineapple
Brightly colored tray, for ice cream cups

PAPER + RIBBON + STRING
Paper cups, for ice cream
Colorful paper pinwheels + clothespins
Thin satin ribbon, to hang pinwheels
Paper streamers
Card stock, for welcome sign
Mexican paper flags
Paper bags

LIGHTING
2 strings of lights
2 pillar candles
5 votive candles

Memorial Day Cookout

On this unofficial first day of summer, we open the pool, enjoy the garden and, of course, celebrate our veterans with family and friends at a cookout. For me, it's also the start of the outdoor entertaining season; I always look forward to the warm weather so that I can push the party outside.

Whenever I can identify a theme for a party I will, and you should, too. This party is a great opportunity to pull out and use all your vintage things for the table décor and plating—think old-fashioned pie tins and wooden utensils and enamelware. It's a perfect theme for this day—a time to reflect, recollect, and to look to the past for inspiration.

In the spring you can always find me in my garden, harvesting everything we can possibly eat, so every-thing on this menu—garden-fresh ingredients, grilled specialties, pickled relishes, and chilled surprises—is inspired by that seasonal harvest. The appetizer uses tiny, tender pea tendrils to decorate the chilled pea soup shooters. The dessert is a blueberry pie (this is the best blueberry pie you've ever had, I swear it!) with a little homemade lavender ice cream.

Even the color palette of red, white, and lavender for the table reflects the beautiful blooms in the garden. You can make use of your own blooms with a lesson in making flower arrangements in this chapter, too. It's not the last lesson in floral arranging—there are more in later chapters. I hope you'll be a pro by the end of this book.

MENU

Chilled Pea Soup Shooters

Blueberry and Arugula Salad
with Sweet Radishes and Homemade Creamy
Italian Dressing

Oven-Baked Polenta with Tomato Sauce

Sun-dried Tomato Grilled Flank Steak
with Pickled Onions

Blueberry Pie with Lavender Ice Cream

CHILLED PEA SOUP SHOOTERS

Makes 10 to 12

These chilled soup shooters remind me of a party I threw several years ago. I matched married couples to specific recipes and we all cooked dinner together. It's really fun to cook together in pairs, but you have to be a good matchmaker when it comes to assigning recipes: Some of your friends may have more skills in the kitchen than others. I gave this super-simple recipe to one of our favorite couples who were not experienced cooks but were willing to try anything. They took their task very seriously and the result was impressive—plus, they had a great time preparing the shooters and were impressed with themselves and the result. What could be more fun than serving them in glass test tubes or shot glasses?

3 cups fresh shelled English peas
3 shallots, coarsely chopped
1/2 cup olive oil, divided
3 tablespoons fresh lemon juice
1/2 tablespoon salt
1 tablespoon chopped fresh thyme leaves
12 sprigs of thyme
Pea tendrils, for garnish

Fill a large bowl with ice water. (This will be used to "shock" the peas after blanching them to stop the cooking and preserve their bright color. Blanching makes vegetables extra crunchy without fully cooking them.)

Bring the peas to a boil in a stockpot with 4 cups water, and continue to boil for 2 minutes. Remove the pot from the heat, drain, and immediately transfer the peas to the bowl of ice water. Allow the peas to completely cool, then drain and set aside at room temperature.

Heat 1/4 cup of the olive oil in a medium sauté pan over low heat. Add the shallots and cook for 5 minutes, stirring often, until they are soft and translucent but not browned.

Combine the peas and shallots in a blender. Add 1 cup water and the lemon juice, salt, and chopped thyme and blend until combined. With the blender still running on low speed, slowly add the remaining 1/4 cup olive oil. Pour the soup into a container, cover tightly with plastic wrap or a lid, and refrigerate for 1 hour, or up to 24 hours, until you are ready to serve. If the soup thickens, stir in a little water to thin it.

To assemble the shooters, use a small teaspoon to spoon the soup into each individual glass. Garnish with a sprig of thyme and a pea tendril. Arrange the shooters in a bucket or tray of ice to keep the soup cold.

How to make
TAGS FOR THE PEA SOUP SHOOTER BUCKET

MATERIALS:

Paper gift tag
Red-and-white baker's twine
Scissors

DIRECTIONS:

Use a pen or colorful marker to write "Chilled Pea Soup Shooters" on a gift tag and use baker's twine to tie it around the bucket.

How to make a
FLOWER BUCKET

MATERIALS:

1 (2-gallon) galvanized bucket
2 bunches white cottage roses
2 bunches lavender flowers
2 bunches purple flowers, your choice
Baker's twine
Scissors

DIRECTIONS:

1. Fill a bucket halfway full with water.

2. Cut the flowers to a length where the flower heads just peek over the edge of the bucket.

3. Arrange flowers so that the colors are mixed.

4. Cut a 3-foot length of baker's twine, wrap the twine around the bucket 2 or 3 times, and tie it in a bow.

BLUEBERRY AND ARUGULA SALAD

with Sweet Radishes and Homemade Creamy Italian Dressing

Serves 4 to 6

I love to serve salad in unexpected vessels, such as an enamel roasting pan. If you display greens in a white bowl, the colors will pop and the textures really read well. White plates and bowls frame a fresh, colorful dish as if it were a piece of art. That's why white plates are the favorite serving choice of chefs and food photographers! A great trick I learned from a chef friend is to toss the vegetables with the dressing first and then add the lettuce and toss again to achieve a perfectly dressed salad.

CREAMY ITALIAN DRESSING

1/4 cup plain Greek-style yogurt
1 shallot, finely chopped
1 garlic clove, grated using a Microplane grater
1/2 cup olive oil
1 lemon, juiced
2 teaspoons chopped fresh thyme leaves
1 teaspoon salt
1/4 teaspoon pepper

SALAD

1 cup blueberries
1 bunch baby radishes, thinly sliced
1/2 small red onion, thinly sliced
4 cups arugula (3 ounces), washed and dried
1/2 cup crumbled feta cheese

For the dressing: Place all the ingredients in a glass jar with a screw top and shake until well combined. The salad dressing will keep, refrigerated, for 2 days.

For the salad: In a large bowl, toss together the blueberries, radishes, and onion with the dressing. Add the arugula and toss again. Sprinkle the salad with the feta cheese and transfer the dressed salad to an interesting serving vessel, such as an enamel roaster, or a flat pan.

OVEN-BAKED POLENTA

with Tomato Sauce

Serves 4 to 6

Serve this creamy polenta hot and steaming on a rustic cutting board, and let guests scoop it up Tuscan-style with big spoons. I first experienced this Italian comfort food presentation many years ago and it's been a part of my party menus ever since.

2 cups coarse-ground polenta or corn grits
1/4 cup olive oil
2 tablespoons salt
1 tablespoon pepper
1/2 cup plus 4 tablespoons grated Parmesan cheese
1 (24–ounce) jar marinara sauce, your favorite brand
1/2 cup chopped fresh Italian parsley

Preheat the oven to 300° F.

In a large bowl, stir together the polenta, 5 cups water, the olive oil, salt, pepper, and 1/2 cup of the grated Parmesan cheese. Pour the polenta mixture into a 3-quart earthenware or glass baking dish and bake, uncovered, for 30 minutes, stirring after 15 minutes. The polenta is done when it is creamy, not firm.

Pour the hot polenta onto a clean, dry cutting board, top with the marinara sauce, and sprinkle with the remaining 4 tablespoons Parmesan cheese and the chopped parsley.

How to make SODA WRAPS

MATERIALS:

12 to 18 (12-ounce) glass soda bottles
1 roll checkered wrapping paper
1 roll red washi tape (decorative Japanese masking tape), available in art stores or giftwrap stores
Scissors

DIRECTIONS:

1. Measure enough checkered paper to wrap around the bottom half of a bottle, plus 1 inch, and cut 3-inch-tall bands that length for each bottle.

2. Wrap a paper band around each bottle to cover the label.

3. Secure the paper where it overlaps using a 1-inch piece of red washi tape.

4. Place a bottle opener and a glass container holding striped straws next to the wrapped bottles, so guests may help themselves.

SUN-DRIED TOMATO GRILLED FLANK STEAK

with Pickled Onions

Serves 4 to 6

This summertime grilled steak recipe is the hands-down family favorite at our house. I like to marinate the steak the night before the party and leave it overnight in the refrigerator. Pickled onions have become a staple in our refrigerator—I use them on sandwiches and salads year-round. They are a great make-ahead treat to have on hand.

MARINADE

1 cup sun-dried tomatoes in oil
5 garlic cloves, peeled
1/4 cup chopped fresh rosemary
2 tablespoons balsamic vinegar
1/4 cup ketchup
1 teaspoon salt
1 teaspoon pepper

1 (3- to 4-pound) flank steak
Pickled Onions (recipe follows)

For the marinade: Combine all the marinade ingredients in the bowl of a food processor and pulse for 1 minute, or until the ingredients form a paste.

Place the steak in a plastic zip-top bag and add the marinade. Seal the bag and massage the marinade over the steak so that it completely coats the meat. Refrigerate the steak for at least 3 hours, or leave overnight. When you are ready to cook the steak, heat a grill to medium-high heat.

Remove the steak from the marinade and pat dry. Grill the steak for 5 to 8 minutes, then turn and continue to grill for 5 to 8 minutes, or until a meat thermometer inserted into the thickest part of the steak reads 130° to 135° F (medium-well). Remove the steak from the grill and allow it to rest at room temperature for 15 minutes. Slice the meat against the grain (the steak should be pink to red inside) into thin slices and serve warm, or at room temperature, with the pickled onions on the side.

PICKLED ONIONS

Makes 1 (12-ounce) jar

These can be made a week ahead and stored in a sealed jar in the refrigerator for up to 2 weeks. This is a quick pickling process, not a canning process.

1 1/2 cups red wine vinegar
1/2 cup sugar
1 teaspoon salt
3 to 5 whole cloves
1 large red onion, cut into 1/4-inch slices

In a saucepan over medium heat, combine the vinegar, sugar, salt, and cloves and simmer for 2 minutes. Add the onion slices and continue to simmer for 10 minutes, then turn off the heat. Remove the saucepan from the heat and allow the onion mixture to cool to room temperature in the pan, then transfer the onions and liquid to a jar. Seal and refrigerate until ready to use.

How to make
NAPKIN ROLL-UPS

MATERIALS:

6 white tea towels or napkins
6 stickers (I like to use rectangular stickers)

DIRECTIONS:

1. Roll each napkin into a tube.

2. Secure each roll with a sticker.

Styling Secrets

SERVING PICKLED VEGETABLES IN A MASON JAR WITH A RUSTIC SPOON OR FORK LETS GUESTS KNOW THE CONTENTS ARE HOMEMADE AND ADDS TO THE VINTAGE APPEAL OF YOUR PARTY.

SERVE SLICES OF THE FLANK STEAK ON A LARGE WHITE PLATTER, OR SOMETHING UNEXPECTED LIKE AN ENAMELWARE DISH. GARNISH WITH FRESH ROSEMARY AND SERVE PICKLED ONIONS OUT OF THE JAR (THIS COULD BE A VINTAGE JAR), WITH A VINTAGE WOODEN-HANDLED FORK.

UNEXPECTED SHAPES AND TYPES OF SERVING VESSELS, SUCH AS SERVING SALAD IN AN ENAMEL PAN, ARE VISUALLY FUN.

BLUEBERRY PIE
with Lavender Ice Cream

Serves 6

This is a delicious blueberry pie recipe, and the addition of the lavender ice cream makes a beautiful combination. Pie is such a comfort food, and I love to plate individual servings in vintage pie tins. I slice a very large piece and serve it to a couple with two forks. This pie crust can be made up to two days ahead of your party and refrigerated until you're ready to bake.

PIE CRUST
2 1/2 cups all-purpose flour

1/4 cup plus 1 teaspoon sugar (for the top crust of the pie)

1/2 teaspoon salt

1 cup (2 sticks) unsalted butter, chilled and cut into 1/2-inch cubes

3 to 4 tablespoons ice water

BLUEBERRY FILLING
4 cups blueberries

3/4 cup sugar

3 tablespoons cornstarch

1/4 teaspoon salt

2 tablespoons unsalted butter, cut in 1/2-inch cubes

3 tablespoons whole milk

Lavender Ice Cream (see recipe opposite)

Fresh lavender sprigs, for garnish

For the crust: Combine the flour, 1/4 cup sugar, and the salt in a food processor, and pulse for 3 seconds. Add the butter and pulse for 20 seconds, or until the dough has formed pea-size pieces. Drizzle the ice water, 1 tablespoon at a time, into the dough and pulse again for 20 seconds, or until the dough is evenly moistened and pulls away from the sides of the bowl.

Turn the dough out onto a work surface and gather it into a ball, turning the dough to catch any dry crumbs. Place the dough on a sheet of plastic wrap and press it into a 1-inch-thick disk. Seal the dough with the plastic wrap and refrigerate for at least 1 hour before using, or up to 2 days if you are making the pie ahead.

For the filling: When you are ready to bake, lightly toss the blueberries in a large mixing bowl with the sugar, cornstarch, and salt and set aside.

Preheat the oven to 425° F.

Halve the dough and form 2 disks. Roll out each pie crust on a lightly floured surface to a 12-inch round. Press 1 dough circle into the pie plate and add the blueberry mixture, mounding the blueberries in the middle. Dot the top of the blueberries with the cubes of butter and cover the pie with the top crust. Trim any excess dough and crimp the two crusts together around the edges of the pie pan using your fingers. Cut 4 slits in the center of the pie to form a circle. Brush the top crust with the milk and sprinkle with the remaining 1 teaspoon sugar. Bake on the bottom rack of the oven for 45 to 50 minutes, until bubbly.

After 20 minutes, or when the top crust is golden, cover the top of the pie with aluminum foil for the duration of the baking time. Allow the pie to cool to room temperature and serve with the Lavender Ice Cream. Garnish slices with sprigs of fresh lavender.

LAVENDER ICE CREAM

Makes 6 cups

3 cups heavy cream

1 cup whole milk

2 tablespoons dried lavender flowers

6 large eggs, plus 2 large egg yolks

1/2 cup sugar

1/4 teaspoon salt

1 teaspoon vanilla extract

1/4 cup honey

Simmer the cream, milk, and lavender in a saucepan over medium-low heat for 10 minutes, or until the milk scalds. Pour the hot milk–lavender mixture into a bowl and let it steep, uncovered, for 30 minutes. Strain the cooled lavender milk back into the saucepan and return to medium-low heat until the milk is hot.

In a medium mixing bowl, whisk the eggs, sugar, salt, and vanilla until creamy. Add 1/4 cup of the hot lavender milk mixture into the egg mixture, whisking continuously as you pour. Add the egg mixture back into the saucepan with the hot milk, bring to a simmer over medium heat, and continue to simmer for 10 to 15 minutes, until the custard is thick enough to coat the back of a metal spoon. Remove from the heat and whisk in the honey.

Transfer the custard to a bowl, cover with plastic wrap, and refrigerate for at least 2 hours, until thoroughly chilled. Put the custard into an ice cream maker and follow the manufacturer's instructions to make the ice cream. Place the ice cream into a loaf pan lined with plastic wrap. Freeze for at least 8 hours and serve.

ELEMENTS

SERVING PIECES
6 white plates
1 ceramic pie dish for baking pie
1 vintage pie tin, for serving
1 ice cream scoop

GLASS
10 to 12 shot glasses or glass test tubes,
for chilled pea soup shooters
1 Mason jar, for pickled onions
12 bottles natural soda, such as Izze brand
Tall vase, to hold straws

WOOD
Small disposable wooden spoons
Wooden cutting board

METAL
Small galvanized bucket, for ice
6 forks, knives, and spoons
Metal or natural basket, to hold flatware and
napkin roll-ups
3 to 6 vintage pie tins, for individual slices of pie
Metal cup, to hold wooden spoons
2 white enamel baking pans, 1 (12 x 10-inch) for
serving the flank steak, and 1 (10 x 8-inch) for
serving the salad
1 serving fork, for the steak
Salad servers
1 fork, for pickled onions
3 spoons, for serving polenta
Pie server
1 large galvanized bucket, for flowers
1 white enamel tray to hold sodas

FABRIC
6 cotton tea towels or napkins
1 red-and-white tablecloth

PAPER + STRING
Red-and-white baker's twine, for
pea soup shooters and flowers
Stick-on labels, for napkin roll-ups
Paper gift tag, to tie on galvanized bucket
Red, white, and blue striped straws
Checkered paper for wrapping soda bottles

FLOWERS
Blossoms in white and lavender
Bunch of fresh lavender, for garnish

Italian Spring Feast of SQUASH BLOSSOMS

I am an avid gardener, maybe even an obsessive one. Those of you who are gardeners will understand that a garden is like a family member—it needs tending and love and it is a continuous source of enjoyment. In late May and early June I start to spot bright yellow flowers popping up in the squash bed. Squash blossoms have become a family favorite at dinnertime in our house—who knew that kids would like to eat flowers? I fry up a bunch and we sit outside under the arbor and eat them until we can't move.

I learned how to make these fragile little packages one summer in Italy when I visited the home of a woman who conducted private cooking lessons in the tiny town of Ravello on the Amalfi coast. While we enjoyed her homemade limoncello liqueur, she taught me the details of stuffing and frying the flavorful flowers. In her teeny kitchen, we stood side-by-side and fried squash blossoms until they made a giant heap on a terra-cotta platter. The melt-in-your-mouth consistency and the smoky cheese surprise in the center made my heart skip a beat. The view from her dining terrace, situated high on a cliff over a deep blue Mediterranean Sea speckled with boats and yachts, was fabulous. We finished off the whole platter of blossoms and moved on to pasta and dessert. I hardly remember walking home. I plopped happily into bed and dreamed, the lessons of the day dancing in my head. This party menu is inspired by that magical night when I learned to cook squash blossoms the Italian way. You will love recreating the Italian celebration of summer's first harvest with this elegant dinner party.

menu

Ricotta-Stuffed Fried Squash Blossoms

Arugula Salad
with Parmesan Shavings, Balsamic, and Lemon Oil

Spaghettini
with Zucchini Coins, Speck, and Truffle Oil

Affogato
with Olive Oil–Vanilla Ice Cream and
Rosemary Biscotti

RICOTTA-STUFFED FRIED SQUASH BLOSSOMS

Serves 4 to 6

When May rolls around and the squash begins to blossom, I'm ready to start stuffing and frying. If you've never tasted fried squash blossoms, the delicate flavors and crisp texture will win you over. This recipe gives you tips to properly prepare this deceptively simple dish. Just be careful not to wash the squash blossoms under the tap—this destroys the texture of the flower. Make sure the oil is very hot; I like to drop a bit of the batter into the oil first to test it—if it quickly crisps up, you're ready to roll. Hot oil is the secret to these delicate nibbles. I guarantee you will be planting yellow squash in your garden next year just to have this cheese-filled delicacy again. You can find squash blossoms in high-end groceries, and seasonally in farmers' markets.

CHEESE FILLING
1 cup whole-milk ricotta, preferably fresh
1 large egg yolk
1/4 cup finely chopped fresh basil
3 tablespoons grated Parmesan cheese
1/2 teaspoon salt

12 to 16 large zucchini squash blossoms

BATTER
1/2 cup all-purpose flour
1 large egg
3 tablespoons grated Parmesan cheese
1 teaspoon salt
1 teaspoon pepper
3/4 cup chilled seltzer or club soda
4 cups vegetable oil, for frying

For the filling: In a medium mixing bowl, stir or use a hand mixer to whip together all the ingredients until thoroughly blended.

Clip the squash blossoms, leaving a 2-inch stem attached. (They will come this way from the grocery.) Wash the squash blossoms gently in a bowl of water, not under the tap, and dry with a paper towel. Carefully force a small opening in the top of each blossom. Fill a piping bag, or a plastic bag with a hole cut into one corner, with the cheese filling and pipe 1 tablespoon of the filling into the opening of each blossom, filling the flower about halfway up the blossom. Grasp the ends of the flower and gently twist closed. You may refrigerate the stuffed blossoms for up to 2 hours, or fry them immediately.

For the batter: Whisk the flour, egg, cheese, salt, and pepper in a medium mixing bowl until the batter is a smooth consistency. Add the seltzer and continue to whisk until well combined.

To fry the squash blossoms, heat the oil in a Dutch oven over high heat until a few drops of batter dropped into the oil crisp up. Use small tongs to dip the stuffed blossoms into the batter, turning to coat, then drop them carefully into the hot oil. Fry batches of 5 blossoms at a time; do not crowd. Fry the blossoms for 5 minutes (no need to turn), or until crisp, and drain on paper towels. Serve hot.

How to
FILL SQUASH BLOSSOMS

DIRECTIONS:

1. Wash the blossoms in a bowl of cold water, and place on a paper towel to air dry.

2. Using your fingers, open the tops of the blossoms enough to pipe in the cheese filling.

3. Fill a piping bag fitted with a 1/2-inch round tip with the cheese filling.

4. Gently pipe 1 tablespoon of filling into each blossom.

5. Using your fingers, twist the top of the blossom shut in a clockwise motion.

6. Dip the stuffed blossoms into the batter, then grasp the stem of the blossoms and gently lower the blossoms into the hot oil. Fry for 5 minutes, or until they are crispy and brown.

ARUGULA SALAD

with Parmesan Shavings, Balsamic, and Lemon Oil

Serves 4 to 6

6 cups arugula

1 cup shaved Parmesan (I use a potato peeler to
  make the shavings)

3 tablespoons good balsamic vinegar

3 tablespoons lemon olive oil (see Source Guide,
  page 222)

1/2 teaspoon salt

Wash and dry the arugula and toss in a large bowl
with the Parmesan shavings. Add the balsamic
vinegar, lemon olive oil, and salt, and toss again.
Serve immediately.

SPAGHETTINI

with Zucchini Coins, Speck, and Truffle Oil

Serves 4 to 6

1 (12-ounce) package dried whole-wheat
  spaghettini

1/4 cup olive oil

2 garlic cloves, minced

1/4 pound (1/2 cup) cubed speck

2 medium zucchini, sliced into coins

1 teaspoon salt

1/2 teaspoon pepper

1/4 cup grated Parmesan cheese

3 tablespoons truffle oil

Fill a stockpot three-quarters full with water and
bring to a boil over high heat. When the water is
boiling, cook the pasta for 10 minutes, or until it is al
dente.

Meanwhile, heat the oil in a large sauté pan over
medium heat and use a Microplane grater to grate
the garlic into the oil. Sauté the garlic for 1 to 2 minutes, then add the speck, zucchini coins, salt, and
pepper, and continue to sauté for 5 to 8 minutes,
turning the speck and zucchini so that they evenly
brown.

Drain the pasta and add it to the zucchini mixture
in the sauté pan. Stir to combine. Transfer to a serving bowl, top with the Parmesan cheese, and sprinkle with the truffle oil.

Serve immediately.

Styling Secrets

DOUBLE UP ON THE TABLE-
CLOTHS FOR A LUXURIOUS
LOOK. LAYERING TABLECLOTHS
LOOKS SO RICH THAT NO ONE
WILL EVER SUSPECT YOUR TABLE
IS A SIMPLE FOLDING TABLE.

USE AN UNEXPECTED ROOM OF
YOUR HOME, LIKE A FOYER OR A
LIBRARY, FOR A MORE INTI-
MATE DINNER PARTY. NO NEED
TO MOVE YOUR DINING TABLE,
JUST USE A FOLDING TABLE AND
DRESS IT WITH WHITE LINENS
AND SPARKLING DINNERWARE.
THINK OF EACH OF YOUR ROOMS
AS A POSSIBLE PARTY VENUE.

ROLL UP THE NAPKINS AND
TIE THEM WITH RED, WHITE,
AND GREEN RIBBON TO ADD
AN ITALIAN THEME TO THE
EVENING.

USE MASSES OF VOTIVE AND
PILLAR CANDLES SET IN MANY
DIFFERENT STYLES OF WATER
GLASSES.

PLACE 3 OR 4 SMALL WATER
GLASSES FILLED WITH YELLOW
FLOWERS DOWN THE CENTER OF
THE TABLE. CUT THE STEMS
SHORT ENOUGH SO THAT THE
FLOWERS JUST SPILL OVER THE
LIP OF THE GLASS. THIS IS A
GENERAL RULE TO ACHIEVING
A PROFESSIONAL LOOK WITH
TABLE ARRANGEMENTS—IT

ALLOWS GUESTS TO TALK EASILY
OVER THE CENTERPIECES AND
IT PUTS FLOWERS IN FRONT OF
EACH GUEST, RATHER THAN
JUST THE GUESTS SEATED AT
THE MIDDLE OF THE TABLE.

AFFOGATO

with Olive Oil–Vanilla Ice Cream and Rosemary Biscotti

Serves 6; makes 3 dozen biscotti

When I first heard about this dessert I was in Italy, eating with my friend and Italian tutor Vincenzo. At the end of our meal he ordered affogato and I asked, "Wait—that's a thing to eat?" You see, affogato means "drowned." He explained that this dessert is drowned in espresso. So I ordered one ... and the angels sang. If you are a coffee lover, this simple combination will make your heart sing, too. I doctor up store-bought vanilla ice cream with olive oil; it adds subtle flavor and a smoother texture. The ice cream can be prepared ahead and frozen, of course. The biscotti will keep for a couple of days in a zip-top bag, so it can be made ahead. Biscotti also make great gifts for guests to take home at the end of the evening. I keep small cloth bags on hand so that I can tuck a few biscotti in for friends to take home.

OLIVE OIL–VANILLA ICE CREAM

2 quarts premium vanilla ice cream, softened

1/2 cup extra virgin olive oil

1 teaspoon sea salt

ROSEMARY BISCOTTI

1 cup almonds

1/2 cup (1 stick) unsalted butter, melted

1 cup sugar

1 tablespoon chopped fresh rosemary

1 teaspoon vanilla extract

1/2 teaspoon salt

3 large eggs

3 cups all-purpose flour

3/4 cup whole-wheat flour

1 1/2 teaspoons baking powder

6 single shots espresso coffee, or 12 ounces espresso-style brewed coffee (A standard measure for a shot of espresso is 2 fluid ounces. You can brew espresso-style coffee and transfer 2 ounces to each espresso maker to serve.)

For the ice cream: Allow the ice cream to soften at room temperature to a creamy consistency, then transfer to a large bowl. Stir in the oil and salt. Place in a plastic container with a lid, and freeze until you are ready to assemble the affogato.

For the biscotti: Preheat the oven to 350° F.

Place the almonds in a single layer on a baking sheet and roast in the oven for 5 to 7 minutes, until toasted and browned, making sure to monitor the almonds closely, as they will burn quickly. Allow the almonds to cool, then chop them and set aside.

Place the melted butter and sugar in the bowl of a standing mixer and mix on medium speed until blended. With the mixer running, add the rosemary, vanilla, and salt. Add the chopped toasted almonds, then the eggs, one at a time. Gradually add both flours and the baking powder and blend until the dough pulls together. Gather the dough into a ball, wrap it in plastic wrap, and refrigerate for 30 minutes, or until it is firm.

Preheat the oven to 350° F.

Working with the chilled dough on a Silpat (a non-stick silicone mat used in baking and the production of candy) or parchment paper, divide the dough in half and shape each half into a thin loaf, each approximately 3 x 12 inches. Place in loaf pans and pat the top of each loaf flat with your hand. Bake for 30 minutes, or until they are lightly browned on top. Maintain the oven temperature.

Let the loaves cool for 20 minutes, then turn out onto a cutting board. Use a serrated knife to cut 3/4-inch-thick slices, cutting at a diagonal angle.

Arrange the biscotti on a baking sheet and bake for another 20 to 30 minutes, until crisp.

The biscotti can be made ahead and stored in an airtight container or zip-top bag for up to 2 weeks. I like to freeze them, then thaw and serve them at room temperature the day of the party. Frozen, they will keep for up to 2 months.

To assemble the affogato, brew 6 shots of espresso coffee and allow the coffee to cool slightly. It should be warm, not hot, when the dessert is assembled. Place 1 scoop of ice cream in each glass, and pour the espresso over the ice cream. Serve immediately.

Scoop the ice cream into individual glasses and place a small espresso maker (a single-serving Moka is an Italian style stove top espresso maker, see Source Guide, page 222) next to each cup of ice cream so guests can pour the warm espresso over their own portion. Serve with biscotti and a tiny spoon.

ELEMENTS

SERVING PIECES
6 small white plates, for squash blossoms
6 salad plates
6 pasta bowls
1 platter, for squash blossoms
1 large serving bowl, for spaghettini
1 large serving bowl, for arugula salad

TEXTILES
1 white tablecloth
1 smaller white tablecloth, with decorative trim to
use as overlay
6 white linen napkins

GLASS
6 water glasses
6 wine glasses
12 drinking glasses of various heights and shapes:
9 for votive candles, 3 for flowers
6 short highball glasses, for affogato

METAL
6 each: small forks, forks, knives, spoons, and
dessertspoons
2 serving forks, for the pasta and
squash blossoms
1 pair salad servers
6 small Italian stovetop espresso makers for dessert
1 tray to hold desserts and espresso makers

PAPER + RIBBON +STRING
6 (12-inch) lengths of red, white, and green satin ribbon,
1/8-inch width, to tie napkin roll-ups

DECOR
3 small bunches of yellow flowers (lilies or
roses are great)
1 (6-foot) folding table

LIGHTING
9 votive candles
3 to 6 pillar candles

WOOD
3 to 6 candleholders, for pillar candles

PALIO CELEBRATION

The Horse Race of Sienna

For centuries in Sienna, Italy, citizens of that city have held a horse race, now run every summer on July 2nd and August 16th, in the Piazza del Campo, an oval piazza in the center of town. Each neighborhood of the city sponsors their own horse and has their own colorful banner. It is wildly popular, and participants sing neighborhood fight songs, and curse competing neighborhoods, as well as wave the banners of their own neighborhood. Eventually they will end up being worn as scarves around the reveler's neck during the race and at neighborhood celebrations. When a rival approaches someone from another neighborhood, they squirt each other with squirt guns and may insult each other's mother—all very Italian and all to great laughter and fun.

However, as the race itself is Sienna's Super Bowl, it is taken very seriously. Rules are strange—the horse can win the race even if the jockey falls off, and the winning horse will attend his neighborhood's celebratory dinner, decked out in flowers, and corralled in the middle of the party. The party revelers feed him, sing to him, and cheer him late into the night.

It is a colorful, beautiful party with songs, color, laughter, and pageantry. Clothes are made specially to reflect the look of medieval Italy, when the race first began. Over the years, I've gathered many banners from the race that I use to decorate my party. You can buy the banners online, or just cut squares of brightly colored fabric or vintage silk scarves by hand instead. (This party décor is an easy party to repurpose as a Kentucky Derby party. If you choose to do this, you can use the silk colors that are worn by the jockeys as your banners.)

Even if you're not watching this colorful, exciting spectacle in person, it's great fun to fly the banners, drink wine, and sing by candlelight, just as the Siennese do on this summer night.

menu

Mussels in White Wine

Caprese Salad Parmesan Crisps
with Tomato Jam

Penne Pasta
with Arrabbiata Sauce

Grilled Whole Salmon
with Lemon, Tomatoes, and Zucchini

Strawberry Tiramisu

*The ancient horse race Palio and
costumed processional in the main
campo of Sienna, Italy.*

MUSSELS IN WHITE WINE

Serves 6 to 8 as an appetizer

Mussels provide the perfect communal meal. Just place the cooking pan directly on the table with slices of French bread and a stack of bowls. Mussels can be bought at most high-end grocery stores and can be refrigerated, uncovered, or in a ventilated plastic bag, for one day. Mussels are alive and need air. They also need to be debearded before cooking. Debearding is the process of removing the beard, or strings, from the mussels. Most mussels have been debearded at the grocery before you buy them; however, if you need to debeard them, the process is easy. Under cold running water, simply pull the beard off and discard it. I like to serve several white wines, and encourage tasting and discussion about the perfect pairing. The Palio party is the perfect occasion for a wine tasting. Encourage friends to bring their favorite whites, then supply labels for the guests to tag with their name, and let the tasting and the discussion begin.

2 tablespoons olive oil
3 tablespoons butter
2 small shallots, diced
2 small garlic cloves, minced
1/4 teaspoon crushed red pepper flakes
3 pounds mussels, scrubbed and debearded
1 cup dry white wine
1 cup marinara sauce, your favorite brand
1/2 cup chopped fresh Italian parsley
1/4 teaspoon salt
1/4 teaspoon pepper
1 French bread baguette

Preheat the oven to 350° F.

Heat the oil and butter in a large, high-sided saucepan or stockpot over medium-high heat. Add the shallots, garlic, and red pepper flakes and sauté for 3 minutes, or until the shallots are translucent. Add the mussels and wine and cook, covered, for 4 to 5 minutes, or until the mussels open. Discard any mussels that do not open. Stir in the marinara sauce, parsley, salt, and pepper. Meanwhile, heat the French bread in the oven for 5 to 7 minutes, then slice and serve warm with the mussels. Let guests serve themselves.

Styling Secrets

CREATE A FLORAL WREATH AS YOUR CENTERPIECE. THEY ARE TRADITIONALLY HUNG AROUND THE NECK OF THE WINNING HORSE IN A RACE.

IF GUESTS BRING THEIR FAVORITE WINE, ASK THEM TO WRITE THEIR NAMES ON THE TAGS AND TIE THEM AROUND THEIR BOTTLES FOR AN IMPROMPTU WINE TASTING. THIS MAKES FOR LIVELY DINNER TABLE DISCUSSION.

ADD A LITTLE "HORSE BARN" CHIC TO YOUR PALIO-THEMED PARTY BY SERVING A MAIN DISH ATOP A LARGE WOODEN CUTTING BOARD AND A RUSTIC PICNIC BASKET.

I LIKE TO USE COLORFUL GLASS VOTIVES AND COLORFUL WATER BOTTLES TO ADD SOME VISUAL EXCITEMENT TO THE TABLE. CHOOSE A COLOR THAT GOES WITH YOUR THEME, AS I HAVE CHOSEN BLUE TO MATCH THE COLORS OF THE BANNERS.

HANG COLORFUL SILK BANNERS ABOVE THE DINNER TABLE. GUESTS WILL FEEL LIKE THEY ARE AT THE PARTY TABLE IN SIENNA, ITALY—OR AT THE KENTUCKY DERBY, IF YOU CHOOSE A MORE LOCAL HORSE RACE TO CELEBRATE.

Suggest that your guests wear colorful silk scarves—each couple can wear the same colors—or order Palio scarves online for your décor (see Source Guide, page 222).

CAPRESE SALAD PARMESAN CRISPS

with Tomato Jam

Makes about 32

These lovely little two-bite morsels are savory and salty with a crunch—perfect to serve with a chilled citrusy glass of Prosecco.

TOMATO JAM
3 tablespoons olive oil
1 garlic clove, chopped
1 teaspoon salt
4 large heirloom tomatoes, coarsely chopped
3 tablespoons sugar
1/2 teaspoon freshly ground black pepper

PARMESAN CRISPS
8 ounces Parmesan cheese, grated (about 4 cups)

TO ASSEMBLE
1 (8-ounce) ball fresh mozzarella, cut into 1/2-inch cubes
1/4 cup thinly sliced fresh basil leaves

For the jam: In a large sauté pan over medium heat, sauté the oil, garlic, and salt for 2 minutes, or until the garlic is golden. Add the tomatoes and sugar and reduce the heat to low. Continue to cook over low heat for 40 minutes, stirring often, until the liquid has completely reduced and the mixture has thickened.

Transfer the jam to a bowl, season with the pepper, and allow the jam to cool completely. This recipe can be made and refrigerated in a lidded jar or covered container for up to 1 week.

For the crisps: Preheat the oven to 375° F.

Drop tablespoon-size mounds of the grated Parmesan cheese onto a parchment-lined baking sheet 2 inches apart, and flatten them slightly with the back of the tablespoon. When baked, these will make 2- to 2 1/2-inch crisps.

Bake for 6 to 8 minutes, or until the crisps are lightly browned. Remove from the oven and allow the crisps to cool for 3 minutes on the baking sheet. Using a spatula, very carefully transfer the crisps to a wire rack (they will be very delicate, so be gentle) and continue baking until all the remaining cheese is used. These crisps can be made 1 day before your party and stored in an airtight container at room temperature.

To assemble: In a small mixing bowl, toss the mozzarella cubes with the basil leaves. Place 1 teaspoon of tomato jam into each Parmesan crisp, then top with 2 teaspoons of the cheese and basil mixture. Plate the crisps on a white tray and serve.

Note: Wait to assemble these until your guests arrive, so that the shells remain crisp.

Choose a roll of brown Kraft wrapping paper with a simple pattern flourish to make an easy table runner. I chose one with a nod to Italian design and décor.

PENNE PASTA

with Arrabbiata Sauce

Serves 6

All'Arrabbiata means "in an angry style" (owing to the heat from the hot peppers) in Italian. This spicy tomato sauce with penne pasta is a classic. This is my version, but feel free to place a small bowl of crushed red pepper flakes on the table, so guests can make their pasta as "angry" as they like.

3 tablespoons olive oil
1/2 yellow onion, chopped
6 garlic cloves, minced
1 (28-ounce) can crushed tomatoes with their juices
1 cup dry red wine
1 teaspoon red wine vinegar
1 1/2 tablespoons sugar
1/2 to 1 teaspoon crushed red pepper flakes
1 teaspoon salt
1/2 teaspoon pepper
1 (4.5-ounce) box dried penne pasta, your favorite brand
2 tablespoons chopped fresh Italian parsley, for garnish
1 cup grated Parmesan cheese, for serving

Heat the olive oil in a large sauté pan over medium heat. Add the onion and garlic and sauté for 3 to 5 minutes, until the onion is translucent. Add the crushed tomatoes with their juices, the wine, vinegar, sugar, red pepper flakes, salt, and pepper. Reduce the heat to low and simmer, uncovered, for 30 minutes, stirring occasionally.

While the sauce is simmering, bring a large stockpot filled halfway with water to a boil and add the box of penne pasta. Stir and continue to boil until the pasta is al dente. Drain the pasta and stir into the sauté pan with the sauce. Transfer the pasta to a large serving bowl and garnish with the chopped fresh parsley. Serve extra crushed red pepper flakes and grated Parmesan cheese on the side.

I found these felt leaves online (*see Source Guide, page 222*) and decided to add them to my party toolbox. They look great with the red and green colors of the Caprese appetizer. You can use green card stock to achieve the same effect by cutting a leaf garland.

GRILLED WHOLE SALMON
with Lemon, Tomatoes, and Zucchini

Serves 6 to 8

Grilling a whole salmon is a crowd event. I love to pull the salmon from the grill and serve it on a large cutting board. Use a basket to elevate the fish and grilled vegetables on your buffet table. It is a visual treat and a great way to feature your main course.

½ cup olive oil

1 tablespoon balsamic vinegar

1 teaspoon coarse salt

1 teaspoon pepper

2 tablespoons chopped fresh thyme leaves

6 lemons, halved

4 medium zucchini, halved lengthwise

6 medium tomatoes, halved

1 (4-pound) whole salmon, filleted

¼ cup capers

1 cup pitted green olives

3 tablespoons lemon olive oil (see Source Guide, page 222), or substitute regular olive oil

Preheat a grill to medium heat.

In a large bowl, stir together the olive oil, balsamic vinegar, salt, pepper, and thyme to make the marinade. Toss the lemon halves and zucchini in the marinade to coat, then remove to a platter. Coat the tomato halves in the marinade and transfer to the platter with the lemon and zucchini.

Place the salmon skin-side down on a sheet of lightly greased, heavy-duty aluminum foil. Brush the salmon with 4 tablespoons of marinade, then grill, covered, for 10 to 15 minutes, until the fish flakes easily. Do not turn.

Grill the zucchini and lemons for 3 to 5 minutes on each side. Grill the tomatoes for 1 to 2 minutes on each side.

Transfer the salmon and vegetables to a large serving platter. If you prefer, cut the zucchini into bite-size pieces, and scatter the capers and olives over the platter. Sprinkle with the lemon olive oil and serve warm or at room temperature.

How to make a
FLORAL WREATH

MATERIALS:

1 (18-inch) Styrofoam wreath, sold at craft stores

1 bunch lemon leaves, available at most grocery stores or your local florist

5 bunches of yellow spray roses

Garden clippers, or a strong pair of scissors

DIRECTIONS:

1. Lay the wreath form on a work surface. Cut the branches of lemon leaves to 4-inch lengths, and stick them into the wreath, all at a slant. Cover the front and the inside and outer edges of the wreath with the leaves. Move clockwise around the wreath, maintaining the same slant to the leaves until the wreath is covered and you can't see the foam form through the leaves.

2. Cut the spray roses to 4-inch lengths and repeat the process, sticking them into the wreath at a slant until the wreath is filled with roses. Note: The wreath should be made no more than 5 hours in advance of the party, in order for the flowers to remain fresh throughout the evening.

STRAWBERRY TIRAMISU

Serves 6

When I am in Italy, one of my favorite places to eat is a very unpretentious beachfront restaurant. The entrées are simple and satisfying and the view is to die for. My favorite thing to order is this dessert— each one is served in an individual French hermetic glass terrine with whipped cream piped into the lid. I was so impressed with the presentation when I ordered it that I serve it the exact same way at home.

2 large eggs, separated
1/4 teaspoon sea salt
1/2 cup sugar
1 cup whipping cream, divided
1 (8-ounce) container mascarpone cheese
1 cup brewed espresso coffee
3 tablespoons Marsala wine
12 crisp ladyfingers, cut in half crosswise
1 cup sliced fresh strawberries
Cocoa powder (optional)

Place the egg whites and salt in the bowl of a stand mixer fitted with a whisk attachment and whisk on high speed until soft peaks form. Transfer to a mixing bowl.

Clean the bowl of the stand mixer and beat the egg yolks and sugar for 2 minutes, or until the mixture is a pale yellow. Add 1/4 cup of the whipping cream and continue to beat for 1 minute. Add the mascarpone cheese and mix on low speed until the custard is a smooth consistency. Remove the bowl from the mixer and fold the beaten egg whites into the custard mixture by hand.

Stir together the espresso and Marsala wine in a small bowl or cup.

Spoon 1/4 cup of the custard mixture into the bottom of each of 6 individual serving vessels. Place 4 pieces of the ladyfingers on top of the custard. Drizzle 1 tablespoon of the espresso mixture over the ladyfingers, then spoon 3 tablespoons of the remaining custard on top of each dessert.

This dessert can be assembled to this point the day before and refrigerated overnight with the lid sealed. Just before serving, open the jar and top each dessert with the sliced strawberries.

Whip the remaining 3/4 cup whipping cream until soft peaks form, and pipe or spoon the whipped cream into the lids of the open jars. Dust the whipped cream with cocoa powder, if desired.

ELEMENTS

SERVING PIECES
6 white plates
Platter, for Caprese crisps
6 colorful small plates
Large serving bowl, for pasta
6 pasta bowls
1 platter, for grilled salmon

WOOD
1 large wooden cutting board

METAL
6 each: forks, knives, and spoons
Paella pan, for serving mussels
1 large serving spoon, for mussels
2 large serving forks, for pasta and salmon
6 small spoons, for dessert
1 bucket, to chill wines

TEXTILES
6 dinner napkins
6 cocktail napkins
3 silk Palio scarves
6 scarves for guest to wear (these can be brightly colored vintage scarves)

GLASS
8 water glasses
12 wine glasses: 6 white wine and 6 red wine
6 French hermetic glass terrines, for tiramisu
3 blue bottles of water

BASKETS
1 bread basket
1 large picnic basket, to use as a table riser for the main dish

DECOR
3 bunches of yellow spray roses
1 bunch of lemon leaves

PAPER + STRING
1 roll of wrapping paper
12 paper labels with strings, for marking wine bottles

LIGHTING
12 blue glass votives, with candles

SUMMER POOL GRILL-OUT

I love pool parties. Growing up in Milwaukee, Wisconsin, no one had a pool—the only pool I knew of was the Brookfield community pool. We had lots of fun there every summer, but it was not exactly a place we could call our own. The idea of throwing a pool party was always intriguing to me, so when we moved to the South and built our house, a pool was a must. A pool party was the first big party we threw in our new home, and it was so fun and easy that we had four more parties that summer! Pool parties are super casual, which makes it fun for everyone. Guests can linger and graze all day on the kinds of simple, fresh—and healthful—foods that make summer so delicious.

I also call this a spa party—you can entertain and lounge at the same time. It's not necessary to have a pool. Set lounge chairs outside and relax with your friends. Invest in some of those bottles with fans that spray water. It's a day to relax, enjoy, and catch some rays.

Normally, I stay away from plastic serving pieces, but this is a day to bring out colorful plastic plates and cups. The big plastic beach balls set the color palette and are really fun to brighten up your table and to just kick around. Buy a bunch of small ones and give them to guests at the end of the party. Choose a fabric tablecloth in a bright color for a rich look.

Use disposable dessert spoons—those little wooden spoons that we used to call ice cream spoons. They're a throwback to our childhood, and what pool party isn't?

menu

Big Fat Greek Salad

Mini Tzatziki Lamb Burgers
with Pita and Cucumber Slaw

Sweet Potato Oven Fries

Limoncello Cheesecake Parfaits

Spa Water

BIG FAT GREEK SALAD

Serves 6

This deconstructed Greek salad is bright and fresh, and it allows guests to serve themselves just the elements they love to make their own. The presentation is perfect for poolside grazing. "Fat" only refers to the size of this salad (I just love the movie—couldn't help it) because it's in fact really healthful yet so satisfying.

SALAD
3 large cucumbers, peeled and cut into 1/2-inch cubes
3 large heirloom tomatoes, cut into bite-size cubes
1/2 medium red onion, thinly sliced
2 (8-ounce) blocks feta cheese, cut
  into 1/2-inch cubes
1 cup pitted Kalamata olives
1 cup whole toasted pine nuts, or substitute
  chopped toasted almonds
1 cup chopped fresh oregano

DRESSING
1/2 cup olive oil
Juice of 1 lemon
3 tablespoons red wine vinegar
2 teaspoons chopped fresh oregano
1 teaspoon salt
1 teaspoon pepper

For the salad: Arrange the salad ingredients in individual rows on a platter.

For the dressing: Whisk the oil, lemon, and vinegar together in a small mixing bowl. Sprinkle with the oregano, salt, and pepper and whisk to blend.

Serve the dressing in individual tiny bowls or glass beakers.

MINI TZATZIKI LAMB BURGERS

with Pita and Cucumber Slaw

Serves 6 to 8

The tzatziki sauce in this recipe is addictive. I like to add 1 teaspoon of salt to the shredded cukes, put them in a strainer, and let them sit for a few minutes before I squeeze out the excess water. You'll get a thicker sauce. Use the same technique for the Cucumber Slaw, too. It's easiest to shred the cucumbers and the veggies for the slaw in the food processor. Serve the Cucumber Slaw in a bowl alongside the burgers for guests to help themselves.

TZATZIKI SAUCE
1 cup plain Greek-style yogurt
1 garlic clove, minced
1/2 teaspoon salt
1/2 cup shredded cucumber, drained
3 tablespoons chopped fresh dill

LAMB BURGERS
1 pound ground lamb
1 pound ground sirloin
2 teaspoons dried oregano
1/2 teaspoon salt
1/4 teaspoon pepper
8 mini pita breads/pockets

For the sauce: Stir the yogurt together with all the other ingredients in a small mixing bowl until well combined. This sauce may be made 2 days in advance and refrigerated in an airtight container until ready to serve.

For the burgers: Preheat a grill to high heat.

Combine the lamb, sirloin, and oregano in a large mixing bowl and use your hands to mix well. Divide the lamb mixture into 6 to 8 small patties, each 1-inch thick. Grill for 3 to 5 minutes on each side. The burgers should be medium to well-done (140° to 150° F) when tested with a meat thermometer. Place each burger in a mini pita, and serve with tzatziki sauce on the side.

CUCUMBER SLAW

Serves 6 to 8

3 tablespoons white or red wine vinegar
2 teaspoons lemon juice
1 teaspoon sugar
1/2 teaspoon pepper
1 1/2 cups shredded cucumber, drained
2 cups shredded carrots
1 cup shredded savoy cabbage
1/2 cup raisins
1/2 cup slivered almonds, toasted
1/2 teaspoon smoked paprika

In a medium mixing bowl, combine 1/2 cup water with the vinegar, lemon juice, sugar, and pepper. Add the shredded vegetables, the raisins, and almonds, and sprinkle with the paprika before serving. This dish can be made in the morning and refrigerated, covered, until ready to serve.

Styling Secrets

SERVE THE SWEET POTATO FRIES IN INDIVIDUAL GLASSES LINED WITH PARCHMENT PAPER. IT LOOKS GREAT AND GUESTS CAN HELP THEMSELVES.

USE A FOLDING TABLE IN THE GARDEN OR BY THE POOL AS YOUR BUFFET TABLE. THE DIY RUNNER MAKES ANY TABLE FUN AND DECORATIVE WITHOUT MUCH EFFORT OR EXPENSE.

USING PLASTIC FOR THIS PARTY REINFORCES THE POOL-PARTY THEME, WITH BRIGHT COLORS AND WHIMSY, AND PLASTIC IS THE BEST MATERIAL TO USE AROUND THE POOL—NO BROKEN GLASS.

If you don't have a pool, a fun decorating idea is to buy a small baby pool, fill it with water, and float beach balls of all sizes.

SWEET POTATO OVEN FRIES

Serves 6 to 8

It's healthier, of course, but the real plus is that baking puts a nice crunchiness into these sweet potatoes.

4 medium sweet potatoes, peeled and cut into 1/2-inch-wide sticks
1/4 cup olive oil
1 teaspoon sea salt
1 teaspoon pepper
Tzaziki Sauce (see recipe, page 104)

Preheat the oven to 425° F.

Peel and cut the sweet potatoes in half lengthwise, then slice each half into 1/2-inch slabs. Lay each slab on its side and cut 1/2-inch sticks.

Combine the sweet potato sticks, olive oil, salt, and pepper in a large zip-top plastic bag. Seal the bag and shake until the sweet potato sticks are fully coated, being careful not to break the potato sticks.

Place the sweet potato fries in a single layer on a large nonstick baking sheet or oversized cookie sheet. Do not crowd the pan—the more room, the crispier the potatoes will become. Bake for 10 minutes, then remove the pan from the oven and shake it to loosen the fries. Turn the fries using a spatula and bake for another 10 to 15 minutes, until browned and crispy. Remove and serve immediately.

Serve with Tzaziki Sauce on the side as a dipping sauce.

LIMONCELLO CHEESECAKE PARFAITS

Makes 10

I am a big fan of lemon curd. This recipe is fresh and easy to prepare and you'll be surprised how big a punch this little splash of lemon delivers. Assemble the desserts in the 2-ounce shot glasses in the morning and refrigerate them until the party. I always make a couple of extra desserts just in case anyone wants seconds.

CHEESE FILLING
1 pound (2 cups) fresh ricotta cheese
2 ounces soft fresh goat cheese, at room temperature
1/4 cup sugar
1/4 teaspoon lemon zest
3 tablespoons limoncello liqueur

GRAHAM CRACKER CRUST
3/4 cup finely ground Graham cracker crumbs
1/4 cup sugar
3 tablespoons unsalted butter, melted

TO ASSEMBLE
1 jar lemon curd, preferably Stonewall Kitchen or Dickinson's

For the filling: Stir together the ricotta and goat cheese in a small bowl until they are creamy and smooth. Add the sugar, lemon zest, and limoncello and whip until blended. Set aside while you make the crust.

For the crust: In a medium mixing bowl, stir together all the ingredients until they resemble blended bread crumbs.

To assemble the individual desserts: Place 1 tablespoon of the cracker crumb mixture into the bottom of a shot glass, add 1 tablespoon of the cheese filling on top, then layer 1 tablespoon of the lemon curd on top of the cheese filling, and repeat the layers until the glass is filled to the top. The top and final layer should be the crumb mixture.

Cover the glasses with plastic wrap and refrigerate for a minimum of 2 hours, or make the dessert in the morning and refrigerate until the party.

SPA WATER

Makes 5 gallons

This super simple idea goes a long way to making your guests feel pampered. I love the idea of creating a spa vibe at your pool party, and so will you.

1 cucumber, peeled and sliced into coins
1 orange, sliced with rind on
1 lemon, sliced with rind on
2 cups mint leaves, rinsed

Combine all of the ingredients with 5 gallons of water in a large glass container. Add 10 cups of ice, and serve immediately.

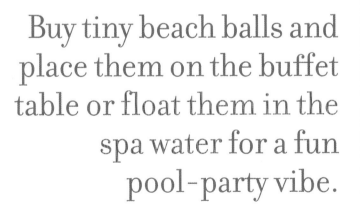

Buy tiny beach balls and place them on the buffet table or float them in the spa water for a fun pool-party vibe.

How to make a

RETRO FABRIC TABLE RUNNER

MATERIALS:

3 (36-inch-width) yards of brightly printed fabric

Pinking shears

DIRECTIONS:

1. Place the fabric on the table to be covered.

2. Trim the fabric with the pinking shears, allowing 5 inches or more of the table on either side of the fabric to be exposed.

3. Allow an extra 6-inch drop of fabric at each end of the table. Trim the ends with the pinking shears.

PLATTERS + SERVING BOWLS

Large white plate, for shot glass desserts

Large platter, for salad

Large platter, for burgers

GLASS

6 to 8 juice glasses, for sweet potato fries

10 (2-ounce) shot glasses, for cheesecake dessert

Oversized jar or pitcher, for spa water

METAL

Folding table (optional), for buffet

TEXTILES

8 napkins

Fabric, for table runner

PAPER + STRING

Parchment paper, for oven fries

WOOD

8 forks

9 spoons, 1 extra for dressing

PLASTIC

8 snack plates

Salad servers

8 plastic cups

1 ladle, for spa water

Medium bowl, to hold extra ice cubes

Small bowl for dressing

2 (12 x 14-inch or 14 x 16-inch) trays

6 large beach balls

16 small beach balls

FOURTH OF JULY PICNIC

The town I grew up in held an amazing fireworks display every Fourth of July. My parents' best friends would drive us in our old Woody station wagon down to sit by Lake Michigan and watch the show. We would have cheeseburgers grilled by friends and then go watch the fireworks. This was the only day of the year I was allowed to eat a cheeseburger because my parents didn't understand that sort of American food. Eating it was heaven, of course! When we got home, we would have apple pie and ice cream, which was an American treat my parents understood. The pie was always from the market, which is the reason I have a store-bought apple pie in this menu. It's for convenience, but it's also a memory that I preserved in my own special way.

If you have a great apple pie recipe that you prefer to use, by all means do so. These party ideas are meant to help you get started creating—as well as continuing—your own traditions with your own unique stamp on them.

Summer is in full swing in early July, so there's more sun each day. That means you'll have more prep time in the morning if the party is planned for late afternoon or early evening. Use the early afternoon to hang the lights and prepare one or two of your final tasks before the party. I love to hang the lights above the picnic table. It is a sweet surprise to see them begin to twinkle once the sun sets.

This menu has evolved over the years since I've moved to the South. Ribs and coleslaw are Southern picnic staples, and there's nothing as good as Southern barbecue. The sweet sauce for the ribs may be a bit messy, but it's delicious, so go ahead and lick your fingers—it's a picnic!

Like cheeseburgers, Woody station wagons, and apple pie, this patriotic celebration is as all-American as it gets, so decorate with vintage finds that have that original Americana feel. Use vintage flags, soda pop and galvanized tubs, and red metal lanterns. If you have them, this is the time to pull out the red-and-white checked metal tray, old picnic baskets, and enamelware.

Corn and Tomato Salad with Fresh Basil

Grilled Peaches with Red Onions

Red, White, and Blue Potato Salad
with Thyme and Rice Vinegar Dressing

Dr. Frank's Favorite Barbecue Ribs

Apple Pie with Vanilla Ice Cream

CORN AND TOMATO SALAD

with Fresh Basil

Serves 6

This brightly colored salad goes great with the barbecue on the menu, and has the advantage of holding up well under the hot sun. I serve any leftovers on pasta: Simply warm the salad, toss with your choice of hot pasta, and pass the Parmesan cheese.

3 cups frozen corn kernels, thawed, or the kernels from 6 cobs freshly cooked corn

2 cups baby tomatoes, halved

1/2 red onion, coarsely chopped

1/2 cup chiffonade (thin ribbons) of fresh basil leaves

2 tablespoons balsamic vinegar

3 tablespoons olive oil

1 teaspoon salt

1/2 teaspoon pepper

In a large bowl, stir together the corn, tomatoes, red onion, and basil.

In a separate bowl, combine the vinegar, oil, salt, and pepper and whisk to blend. Pour the dressing over the vegetables and gently toss to coat. This salad may be prepared a day ahead; cover with plastic wrap and refrigerate overnight.

GRILLED PEACHES

with Red Onions

Serves 6

Grilled fruit is a terrific side dish that is often overlooked by outdoor cooks. The slivers of red onion are a milder alternative to yellow onions, and add a nice crunch to the sweetness of the fruit. You can substitute plums or figs if you prefer.

6 large ripe peaches, pitted and quartered

3 tablespoons olive oil

1/2 small red onion, sliced

6 tablespoons balsamic vinegar

1 teaspoon flaky salt

1 teaspoon freshly cracked black pepper

Preheat a grill to medium heat.

In a large mixing bowl, toss the peaches with the olive oil. Grill the peaches for 5 minutes on each side, or until the fruit has caramelized. Transfer the grilled peaches to a large serving platter and place them cut-side up to show grill marks. Sprinkle with the sliced onion, balsamic vinegar, salt, and cracked pepper and serve immediately.

How to make

NAPKIN WRAPS

MATERIALS:

6 white napkins

6 (4 1/8 x 9 1/2-inch) red envelopes

1 sheet navy 2 1/2-inch round labels

1 strand of vintage Christmas tinsel

Pinking shears

Scissors

DIRECTIONS:

1. Using pinking shears, cut off the top 2 inches and the bottom 2 inches of each envelope to form a sleeve to place the folded napkin into.

2. Fold each napkin to fit into a sleeve; there should be about 1 1/2 inches of the napkin sticking out on either end.

3. Cut a 1/2-inch piece of tinsel and tie around the middle of the sleeve in a knot.

4. Place a navy label onto the knot.

Styling Secrets

ELEVATE YOUR BUFFET DISHES ON CAKE PLATES AND VINTAGE OR ENAMEL TINS.

RED LANTERNS WITH CANDLES LOOK GREAT ON THE BUFFET TABLE AND ILLUMINATE IT WHEN THE SUN GOES DOWN.

ASSEMBLE A BUCKET OF SPARKLERS USING A SMALL ENAMEL BUCKET HALF FILLED WITH SAND. PLACE A BOUQUET OF SPARKLERS INTO THE SAND AND ADD A CUTE CHALKBOARD SIGN THAT SAYS, "LIGHT UP THE FOURTH."

RED, WHITE, AND BLUE POTATO SALAD

with Thyme and Rice Vinegar Dressing

Serves 6

This is a colorful potato salad, perfect for a patriotic party. I suggest placing the salad bowl into a larger bowl filled with ice to assure that the salad stays chilled throughout the party.

1 pound purple potatoes, peeled and halved or
    quartered
2 teaspoons salt
1/4 cup mayonnaise
1 tablespoon chopped fresh thyme leaves
1 tablespoon chopped fresh chives
1 celery rib, finely chopped
1 tablespoon fresh lemon juice
1 tablespoon rice vinegar
1 teaspoon salt
1 teaspoon pepper
1 large red bell pepper, cut into 1/4-inch pieces
1 (14-ounce) can artichoke hearts, drained and
    cut into bite-size pieces

Put the potatoes in a stockpot and fill with enough water to cover the potatoes. Add the salt and bring the water to a boil over high heat. Continue to boil the potatoes for 15 minutes, or until they are fork tender yet firm. Drain and set aside to allow the potatoes to cool while you prepare the dressing.

Stir together the mayonnaise, thyme, chives, celery, lemon juice, rice vinegar, salt, and pepper in a small bowl.

Transfer the cooled potatoes to a large mixing or serving bowl, along with the red peppers and artichoke hearts. Add the dressing and gently toss to coat. Refrigerate, covered, until ready to serve. This salad can be made ahead and refrigerated, covered, overnight.

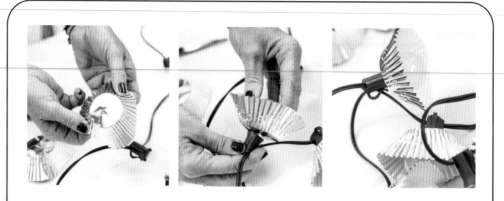

How to STRING SILVER LIGHTS

MATERIALS:

1 (15-foot) strand of patio lights, with clear removable bulbs
15 silver cupcake liners
Scissors

DIRECTIONS:

1. Unscrew the lightbulbs and set aside.

2. Cut a slit with scissors in the middle of each cupcake liner to form a 1/2-inch X big enough to fit the stem of the bulb.

3. Slip the cupcake liner far enough over the stem of each bulb so that it doesn't cover the screw threads.

4. Screw the bulbs with the liner covers back into their sockets.

Use a smaller bowl nestled into a larger, ice-filled bowl for the potato salad. It works both aesthetically and functionally, keeping the salad cold for most of the party.

DR. FRANK'S FAVORITE BARBECUE RIBS

Serves 6

It is true that in the South we love our pork ribs. This version with blueberry jam and smoked paprika creates a lovely sweet-and-smoky combination. My husband, Frank, or "Dr. Frank," as he's known, loves barbecue—I swear it's why we moved to the South. So this is a version I created for my sweet hubby.

A little secret: Because we are Jewish we usually stay away from pork. Frank so loves an occasional barbecue pulled-pork sandwich that he made up a code word for pork—"meat." So pork in our house is called "meat." That Dr. Frank is clever.

1/2 cup (packed) brown sugar
1/2 cup blueberry jam
1 tablespoon smoked paprika
2 teaspoons salt
1 teaspoon ground white pepper
1 teaspoon crushed red pepper flakes
2 garlic cloves, minced
2 cups barbecue sauce (bottled or homemade)
4 pounds baby-back-style pork ribs

In a saucepan over medium heat, stir together all the ingredients except the ribs, bring the sauce to a simmer, and continue to cook for 10 minutes, stirring often. Remove the saucepan from the heat and allow the sauce to cool on the stovetop while you prepare the pork ribs.

You will need to peel the membranes off the ribs. You can have your butcher do this, or you can do it yourself. Slide a small sharp knife under the silver skin, or membrane, move it sideways along the length of the ribs, then grab the loosened skin with a paper towel and remove it.

Combine the ribs with half of the cooled sauce in a large zip-top plastic bag. You may need several bags to hold the ribs; if so, divide the sauce into equal parts per bag. Seal the bags and massage the sauce to cover the meat and marinate in the refrigerator for at least 3 hours. Reserve the remaining half of the sauce for basting on the grill. Preheat a grill to low heat.

Remove the marinated ribs from the plastic bags and discard the marinade in the bags. Wrap the ribs in heavy-duty aluminum foil and seal the edges, making several sealed packages. Place the aluminum foil packages on the grill and cook for 45 minutes, turning the packages every 10 to 15 minutes. Be careful not to let them burn. Remove the ribs from the grill, then remove the ribs from the packages and set aside.

Increase the heat on the grill to medium. Place the ribs directly on the grill, and cook for another 15 to 20 minutes, basting with sauce generously every 2 to 3 minutes, until the meat is evenly browned and caramelized. Serve warm.

How to make a RIBBON RUNNER

MATERIALS:

1 (50-inch-wide) roll of white paper
40 feet of 3/4-inch-wide ribbon, your choice of patriotic pattern
1 roll double-sided clear tape

DIRECTIONS:

1. Roll the white paper out onto your table.

2. Trim the edges of the paper so that there remains a 4-inch drop on each side of your table.

3. Fold the paper over the edge of the table on all sides, forming a crease, so the paper lays flat on the table and won't shift.

4. Measure and cut 3 lengths of ribbon equal to the length of the tablecloth.

5. Evenly space the 3 ribbons down the center of the table.

6. Measure and cut 3 lengths of ribbon equal to the width of the table.

7. Weave the shorter lengths of ribbon over and under the longer lengths, forming a wide basketweave pattern.

8. Secure all of the ends of the ribbon onto the tablecloth with 1-inch pieces of double-sided clear tape.

APPLE PIE
with Vanilla Ice Cream

This is a great opportunity to buy a ready-made dessert from a local bakery and pair it with cleverly presented vanilla ice cream in glass jars.

I like to make special take-away containers for individual slices (see DIY below) and put lidded jars of ice cream on ice for guests to enjoy at the party or take to the fireworks display that evening.

How to make
TAKE-AWAY PIE BOXES

MATERIALS:

8 (8½ x 11-inch) pieces Kraft card stock
1 roll parchment paper
Red-and-white baker's twine
1 store-bought apple pie (Tip: It is easier to slice pie if you place it in the freezer for an hour.)
6 disposable wooden forks (see Source guide, page 222)
Scissors
Tape
Pencil
Ruler

DIRECTIONS:

1. Download the template at www.ajphotostylist.net/

2. Trace the pie container template onto the card stock with a pencil. Trace as many pie containers as you will need.

3. Cut out the pie container.

4. Fold and tape the container into a triangle with a lid, following the template.

5. Cut a 6 x 6-inch square of parchment paper for each container.

6. Cut the apple pie into pieces that fit into the containers (you will need to measure the slice of pie to fit the container, keeping in mind that you need extra room for the pie slice to be wrapped with paper). Fold a crease into the center of each piece of parchment.

7. Unfold and lay the parchment flat, and place a piece of pie on the center crease you have created. Fold the long ends around the slice, then tuck the short ends underneath to form a wedge-shaped package.

8. Place the packaged pie into the brown craft cardboard container.

9. Secure each container with baker's twine and tie a wooden fork into the bow on top of the container. Stack in a basket for guests to take home or eat at the party.

ELEMENTS

SERVING PIECES
6 dinner plates

PLATTERS + SERVING BOWLS
1 medium bowl, for potato salad
1 large bowl, for potato salad ice bath
1 large bowl, for corn salad
3 cake stands, for risers

GLASS
6 (3-inch high) jelly jars, for serving ice cream with pie

METAL
3 trays
3 serving spoons
2 serving forks: 1 for the ribs, 1 for the peaches
6 sets flatware
1 small bucket, to hold napkin rolls
1 tub, filled with ice

TEXTILES
1 large American flag
6 napkins

BASKETS
1 picnic basket

CANDLES + ILLUMINATION
3 (15-foot) strings of lights
6 boxes of sparklers

WOOD
6 each: wooden forks and spoons
Chalkboard or small sign for the sparkler bucket

PROPS + CRAFTS
1 strand of vintage Christmas tinsel
1 (5-inch-diameter) red enamel bucket
1 small sign for sparkler bucket
1 small bag of sand, for sparkler bucket

PAPER + STRING
1 pack silver cupcake liners
6 (4⅛ x 9½-inch) red envelopes
1 sheet (2-inch-round) blue stickers
1 (50-inch-wide) roll of white paper
40 feet of ¾-inch-wide ribbon
Red-and-white striped baker's twine
6 (8 x 11-inch) pieces heavy-weight card stock

RETRO RIVIERA PARTY

I am very blessed to live on the Italian Riviera every summer. We bought a flat in a little seaside town about ten years ago. Everything about our town is splendidly retro, like a village stuck in time; it's the thing I love most about it. The Italians' fascination with the glamour and glitz of the 1960s is still in full swing. Each evening we wander into town and have the traditional Italian apperitivi.

We order refreshing cocktails made with Campari and find a seat with views of both the street and the waterfront. My favorite part of this nightly ritual is the little nibbles that accompany each cocktail. The combinations are creative and satisfying. Sometimes apperitivi becomes dinner as we linger for hours with friends, just people-watching, telling stories, and laughing.

This party is included because apperitivi is a lifestyle choice that I think Americans need to adopt as a way to slow down our frantic lives. Give this party a whirl, and you'll begin to see how apperitivi can become habit-forming. Remember to add a retro Riviera music playlist and a basket of sleek '60s sunglasses for your guests to make the party come to life.

Even if you've never been to Italy, I'm sure you'll recognize the Riviera from those old Italian movies starring Marcello Mastroianni and Sophia Loren. I'm channeling my inner Sophia Loren in this party. Sunglasses and Campari for everyone!

menu

Warm Marinated Olives in Hot Peppers

Prosciutto-Wrapped Breadsticks

3 Signature Cocktails

Italian Chopped Salad

Pasta Frutti di Mare

Calamari Salad in Pesto Oil

Mini Frittatas with Tomato–Red Pepper Coulis

Herb-Roasted Shrimp and Tomatoes

Campari-Orange Sorbet with Pignoli Cookies

WARM MARINATED OLIVES IN HOT PEPPERS

Serves 6

Serve these in individual cups or glasses for guests to pick up. Olives can be tricky to serve. Do you put out a big bowl that everyone dips their fingers into? If so, then what do you do with the pits? This serving suggestion gives guests their own olives and a cup to dispose of the pits. And, oh yes, if you haven't had warm olives, you're in for a surprising treat.

4 cups mixed olives, such as niçoise, Kalamata, and Castelvetrano
2 teaspoons crushed red pepper flakes
5 whole garlic cloves, peeled
2 bay leaves

In a medium sauté pan over medium-low heat, warm the olives, red pepper flakes, garlic, and bay leaves in the oil from the olives for 3 to 5 minutes. Transfer the warm olives to serving vessels and discard the bay leaves and garlic. Serve immediately.

PROSCIUTTO-WRAPPED BREADSTICKS

Serves 6

I always keep prosciutto on hand in the refrigerator because it makes a quick appetizer for guests who pop in. Simply wrap it around breadsticks for a great presentation.

¼ pound good-quality prosciutto, sliced paper-thin and torn into long strips
12 to 18 large breadsticks

Starting at the top, wrap each breadstick with a slice of prosciutto, leaving the bottom half of the breadstick unwrapped. If the prosciutto is sliced paper-thin, it will adhere to the breadstick. Serve immediately.

LIME-Y-THYME-Y GIN

Makes 1 cocktail

In my opinion, handing each person a cocktail as they enter the party is the very best way to greet guests. It gives you a chance to say hello and sets the tone for this cocktail party. Give guests a tour of the nibbles you have set out and introduce everyone. Having a successful party may come down to serving the perfect cocktail, which is why I've included three that fill the bill. You will have your own favorites to add, but try these time-tested classics.

1¼ ounces Bombay Sapphire gin
1 ounce fresh lime juice
1 ounce Thyme Simple Syrup (see recipe, below)
1 thin slice lime
1 sprig fresh thyme

Pour the gin, lime juice, and thyme syrup into a martini shaker half-filled with ice cubes. Shake well. Strain the mixture into a cocktail glass and garnish with a slice of lime and a fresh sprig of thyme.

Thyme Simple Syrup

Makes 2 cups, enough syrup for 16 cocktails

8 sprigs of fresh thyme
2 tablespoons lime zest
2 tablespoons fresh lime juice
1 cup sugar
1 cup water

Combine all the ingredients in a small saucepan over medium heat and bring to a simmer. Cook, stirring occasionally, for 10 minutes. Remove from the heat and allow the syrup to cool. The syrup will keep in a lidded container, refrigerated, for up to 2 weeks.

THE AMERICANO

Makes 1 cocktail

2 ounces Campari
2 ounces Martini and Rossi Rosso vermouth
Splash club soda
1 slice orange

Fill a highball glass with ice cubes, pour the Campari and vermouth over the ice, add a splash of club soda, and garnish with an orange slice.

DRY MARTINI

with Olives

Makes 1 cocktail

3 ounces high-quality gin (I prefer Beefeater), at room temperature
Splash dry vermouth
2 large green olives

Chill a martini glass. Fill a martini shaker half-full with ice cubes and add the gin. Shake well. Swirl a splash of vermouth in the chilled martini glass, strain the chilled gin into the glass, and add 2 large olives on a toothpick as garnish.

ITALIAN CHOPPED SALAD

Serves 6

Using the soft-boiled egg yolks to complete the salad makes a creamy, wonderful dressing. This chopped salad also works as a main course for lunch.

SALAD

2 bunches romaine lettuce

1/4 pound speck, cut into small dice (about 1 cup)

2 tablespoons olive oil

3 eggs

1 bunch radishes, cut into small dice

1/2 red onion, finely chopped

DRESSING

3 anchovies packed in olive oil

2 garlic cloves, minced

2 teaspoons Dijon mustard

Juice of 1 lemon

1/4 cup grated Parmesan cheese

1/2 teaspoon pepper

1/4 cup olive oil

For the salad: Wash and pat the lettuce dry with paper towels. Chop, then wrap the lettuce in a dishtowel, and refrigerate for 30 minutes, or until the lettuce is crisp. Fry the speck in the oil in a sauté pan over medium heat for 3 to 5 minutes, until crispy. Drain on paper towels and set aside.

For the dressing: Use the back of a fork to rub the anchovies over the inside of a wooden salad bowl, mincing them in the process. Add the garlic, mustard, lemon juice, Parmesan cheese, and pepper and stir well. Slowly drizzle the olive oil into the dressing, whisking constantly with a fork.

Place the eggs in a saucepan over medium heat with enough water to cover, and simmer for 3 to 4 minutes. Do not allow to boil. Remove them from the pan of water and peel them under lukewarm running water.

Add the lettuce, speck, radishes, and onion to the bowl with the dressing and toss to coat.

Place the soft-boiled eggs on a cutting board, cut them in half, and place them upside-down onto the salad, so that the soft yolk oozes over the salad. Do not toss this salad. As people serve themselves the yolk will incorporate into the salad. Serve immediately.

PASTA FRUTTI DI MARE

Serves 6 to 8

The name of this dish means "fruits of the sea." It's a must for this Riviera party. I like to serve it in a large white bowl to highlight the beauty of the seafood.

1 (16-ounce) package spaghetti

4 garlic cloves, minced

1 shallot, finely chopped

1/4 cup olive oil

2 tablespoons butter

1/2 cup dry white wine

1/4 cup clam juice

Juice of 1 lemon

1 teaspoon sea salt

1 teaspoon ground white pepper

2 pounds mussels, debearded and scrubbed

2 pounds clams, scrubbed

1 pound cleaned squid (buy squid already cleaned and ready to cook)

1 pound shrimp, peeled and deveined

3 tablespoons crushed red pepper flakes

Fill a stockpot three-quarters full with water and bring to a boil over high heat. When the water is boiling, cook the pasta for 10 minutes, or until it is al dente. Drain the pasta and set aside.

In a separate large pot over medium-high heat, sauté the garlic and shallot in the olive oil for 3 to 5 minutes, until they are translucent. Add the butter, white wine, clam juice, lemon juice, salt, and pepper and stir to combine. When the liquid begins to simmer, lower the heat to medium and add the mussels and clams to the pot first, then the squid and shrimp. Do not stir. Cover and cook for 6 to 8 minutes, until the mussels and clams open and the shrimp is pink. Add the cooked pasta to the pot and toss with the seafood. Turn the heat to low and simmer uncovered for 2 minutes, or until the liquid has reduced by half. Transfer to a serving bowl, sprinkle with the crushed red pepper flakes, and serve warm.

Using large shells as serving pieces is an inexpensive nod to the seaside theme, and you can also find bowls with shell designs on them to complement the theme.

CALAMARI SALAD
in Pesto Oil

Serves 6

This recipe is something that we eat in Italy all summer. Our little beach town on the Riviera has mastered preparing squid, or calamari. Be careful not to overcook the squid—you want them to be tender and overcooking toughens them. This recipe is best made the morning of the party. Refrigerate until an hour before the party, then allow the salad to come to room temperature before you serve it.

2 medium white potatoes, peeled and cut
   into 1-inch cubes (about 2 cups)
3 tablespoons olive oil
4 pounds squid, ink sac removed (ask your
   fishmonger to do this), and sliced into
   3/4-inch rings
1/4 cup pine nuts
1 cup chopped fresh basil leaves
2 garlic cloves
1 teaspoon salt
1/3 cup extra virgin olive oil

Preheat the oven to 350° F.

Place the cubed potatoes in a pot with enough water to cover. Bring to a boil over high heat and boil for 5 minutes. The potatoes should be fork tender. Drain the potatoes and set aside to cool.

Heat the regular olive oil in a sauté pan over medium heat. Add the squid in batches and sauté for 6 to 8 minutes, turning to cook evenly. Do not overcook. Test to make sure the calamari is tender to the bite. Remove from the heat and set aside.

Place the pine nuts on a cookie sheet and toast in the oven for 5 minutes. Make sure to watch closely because pine nuts can burn easily.

In the bowl of a food processor fitted with a steel blade, combine the basil leaves, garlic, toasted pine nuts, and salt. Pulse for 2 minutes, or until a paste forms, then transfer the paste to a large mixing or serving bowl. Add the extra virgin olive oil and stir well. The pesto should be oily. Toss the cooled squid and potatoes in the pesto oil.

Cover the bowl with plastic wrap and allow the calamari and potatoes to marinate, refrigerated, for at least 3 hours. An hour before serving, remove from the refrigerator and allow the salad to come to room temperature.

MINI FRITTATAS
with Tomato–Red Pepper Coulis

Serves 6

Frittatas are a fantastic egg dish, very similar to an omelet except the preparation starts on the stovetop and is then baked in the oven. In this version, the cooking happens entirely in the oven. The coulis is a flavorful tomato sauce that's a perfect accompaniment to this bite-size nibble. This is a super easy and impressive appetizer that takes only minutes to make and tastes great warm or at room temperature.

TOMATO–RED PEPPER COULIS
1 (8-ounce) jar sun-dried tomatoes packed
   in oil, drained
1 small heirloom tomato, cubed

1/2 cup roasted red pepper (1 large pepper
   roasted), or substitute store-bought roasted
   peppers in water, drained
1 small garlic clove
2 tablespoons olive oil

FRITTATAS
5 large eggs
1 cup whole milk
1 cup fresh basil, chopped
1/2 cup shredded Parmesan cheese (shredded
   using a box grater)
2 whole anchovies packed in olive oil, smashed
3 tablespoons olive oil, plus extra for greasing
   the muffin pan
1 large shallot, chopped

For the coulis: Combine all the ingredients in the bowl of a food processor fitted with a steel blade. Pulse for 1 minute, or until the ingredients have formed a smooth sauce. Transfer to a bowl or lidded container, cover, and store at room temperature until you are ready to serve over the frittatas.

For the frittatas: Preheat the oven to 350° F.

In a medium mixing bowl, whisk together the eggs, milk, basil, cheese, and anchovies. Set aside.

Heat the olive oil in a small saucepan and sauté the shallot for 3 to 5 minutes, until it is translucent. Add the shallot to the egg mixture and stir just to combine.

Grease a 12-cup muffin pan with olive oil and fill each muffin cup three-quarters full with the egg mixture. Bake for 20 minutes, or until the frittatas are firm to the touch.

Allow the frittatas to cool to room temperature in the muffin pan, then use a knife inserted into the side of each cup to loosen them, and transfer to a serving dish. Transfer the frittatas to a serving platter or individual plates. Spoon 2 teaspoons of the coulis atop each frittata and serve.

HERB-ROASTED SHRIMP AND TOMATOES

Serves 6 to 8

This is a very versatile recipe. You could toss the roasted shrimp and tomatoes with fresh pasta and a little feta cheese, or serve over grilled artisan bread for a family dinner option. I like to serve this appetizer in a pretty bowl on a buffet, with a stack of small plates for guests to help themselves. Time this dish to be in the oven when guests begin to arrive, and you'll have an appetizer to serve immediately.

2 pounds (21 to 25 count) shrimp, peeled and
   deveined
1 pint cherry tomatoes, halved
3 tablespoons chopped fresh Italian parsley, divided
1 tablespoon chopped fresh oregano
2 teaspoons chopped fresh rosemary
2 garlic cloves, minced
1 teaspoon coarse sea salt
1/4 teaspoon crushed red pepper flakes (optional)
1/4 cup olive oil
1 lemon, cut into wedges, for garnish

Preheat the oven to 350° F.

In a large mixing bowl, combine the shrimp with the tomatoes, 2 tablespoons of the parsley, the oregano, garlic, salt, and red pepper flakes (if using). Add the olive oil and toss to coat. Spread the shrimp and tomatoes in a single layer on a large, rimmed baking sheet. Bake for 16 minutes, turning the shrimp and tomatoes halfway through, until the shrimp turns pink. Transfer to a serving bowl and garnish with the remaining chopped parsley and the lemon wedges. Serve warm or at room temperature.

CAMPARI-ORANGE SORBET

Serves 6 to 8

If you love Campari (a popular bitter Italian liqueur that is an acquired taste), I know you'll like this recipe. But if you don't like Campari, or have never tried it, then you really must give it a try in this sorbet. It is delicious, and has none of the bitterness of the liqueur. Make the sorbet the day before the party so that it has time to chill properly in the freezer.

The Pignoli Cookies (see recipe opposite) are a perfect accompaniment.

1 cup sugar
Zest of 3 oranges (use a Microplane)
3/4 cup Campari
2 cups freshly squeezed orange juice

In a small saucepan, combine the sugar and orange zest with 1 cup water, and bring just to a boil over high heat. Remove from the heat and allow the simple syrup to cool in the pan. Add the Campari and orange juice to the syrup and stir to combine. Transfer to a container with a lid and refrigerate for a minimum of 1 hour, until very cold.

Transfer the Campari mixture to an ice cream maker and follow the manufacturer's instructions to make the sorbet. Spoon the sorbet into a loaf pan lined with plastic wrap and freeze overnight.

Note: The sorbet will be soft because of the alcohol content of the Campari. Freeze the sorbet overnight before you serve.

PIGNOLI COOKIES

Makes 2 dozen

The recipe for these cookies started with an old friend's Italian grandmother. Many years ago, she wrote down only the ingredients—with no measures—on a tiny piece of paper. I took it from there and have honed it over the years.

2 1/4 cups pine nuts, divided
1/4 cup olive oil, plus 1 teaspoon for coating your hands
1/2 teaspoon salt
1 cup sugar
1 cup all-purpose flour
2 egg whites, beaten

Preheat the oven to 325° F.

Arrange 1 cup of the pine nuts on a baking sheet lined with a Silpat or parchment paper, and toast in the oven for 3 minutes, or until they turn a caramel brown color, watching closely to prevent burning.

Remove the toasted pine nuts from the oven, leaving the oven on to maintain temperature, and set the pine nuts aside to cool to room temperature.

Combine the toasted pine nuts, 1/4 cup of the olive oil, and the salt in the bowl of a food processor and pulse until the mixture forms a paste, about 1 minute. Add the sugar, flour, and egg whites to the bowl of the food processor and pulse for 30 seconds, or until a soft dough forms.

Increase the oven temperature to 350° F.
Line 2 baking sheets with parchment paper. Place the remaining 1 1/4 cups pine nuts in a single layer on a large plate.

Rub 1 teaspoon olive oil onto your hands to coat them. Scoop up a rounded teaspoonful of the cookie dough and roll it into a ball using your hands, then roll the ball in the pine nuts, coating all sides.

Place the cookies 2 inches apart on the prepared baking sheets. Bake for 20 to 22 minutes, until golden brown. Remove from the oven and allow the cookies to cool in the pan.

The pignoli cookies can be made a day ahead and stored in a zip-top plastic bag.

Shot glasses with small spoons double as containers for frozen desserts. Fill them with ice cream and freeze the individual servings ahead of time, so that you only need to add a cookie and—voila!—dessert is served.

Styling Secrets

LARGE VASES FILLED WITH SHELLS AND PALM FRONDS CREATE DRAMA AND A COASTAL, MEDITERRANEAN AMBIANCE.

BY ADDING INEXPENSIVE FABRIC POUF OTTOMANS AROUND THE ROOM OR ON YOUR PATIO, YOU CAN ACHIEVE AN INSTANT RIVIERA LOUNGE VIBE.

SET OUT A CONTAINER OF OVERSIZED RETRO SUNGLASSES FOR GUESTS TO WEAR DURING THE PARTY. CREATE A SIGN THAT SAYS, "TAKE A PAIR."

HUNT FOR OLD HIGHBALL GLASSES AT LOCAL FLEA MARKETS. YOU'LL USE THESE FOR PARTIES AGAIN AND AGAIN.

take a pair!

How to make
SHELL VASES

MATERIALS:

1 package (4 cups) of assorted shells,
   available at craft stores
2 palm fronds (you can buy palm fronds at
   a floral shop; if they aren't stocked they
   can special order them for you)
1 large spray of fresh orchids
1 large clear glass vase, at least 20 inches high

DIRECTIONS:

1. Place 2 cups of the shells in the bottom of
the vase.

2. Add the palm fronds and the orchids.

3. Pour in the rest of the shells.

4. Fill with enough water to reach halfway
up the vase.

MUSIC = AMBIANCE

*Music is an important but often forgotten element
of a party. I love to pick a playlist that reflects the
theme of the party and the ambience I want to create. And these days, adding different choices of
music has never been easier.*

*I like to use Pandora or iTunes, or even just tune
in to one of my television cable music channels—
it's not necessary to invest in great speakers or
sound systems if you don't already have them.
Choose a playlist that works with your party
theme, and remember to make it lively. There is
nothing worse than a sleepy playlist—sleepy songs
make for sleepy guests.*

SERVING PIECES
2 large spoons, for calamari salad, tomatoes, and shrimp
1 large fork, for seafood pasta
1 small tray, for dessert shot glasses
Salad tongs

PLATTERS + SERVING BOWLS (all white)
Large platter, for calamari salad
1 large bowl, for seafood pasta
1 medium bowl, for roasted shrimp and tomatoes
1 medium shallow bowl, for chopped salad

GLASS
16 highball glasses
8 martini glasses
Large glass cylinder, for candles
8 tall glasses, for olives
8 tall glasses, for breadsticks
2 vases, for sunglasses
8 small shot glasses, for sorbet
Small bottle, for salad dressing

METAL
1 sign holder, for sunglass display
16 small forks
Martini shaker
16 small spoons, for dessert

TEXTILES
4 fabric poufs, for seating
16 assorted linen cocktail napkins (blue-and-cream
or -white pattern)

PAPER + STRING
1 piece of card stock, for sunglass sign

CANDLES + ILLUMINATION
Votive candles, with holders
1 large pillar candle Candelabra, or tall candlesticks

WOOD
1 tray, for cocktails
20 decorative wood picks

PLASTIC
1 aqua tray
8 square coasters, for serving frittatas
16 small plates

PROPS + CRAFTS
Coral (available at most craft stores)
Sea fan (available at most craft stores)
Assorted small vases and shells to decorate the table

FLOWERS
1 large spray of orchids 4 palm fronds

WINE HARVEST
Party

There's something so appealing about having a wine harvest dinner. It conjures many lovely images: the beauty of the vineyards, the connection to the land, and, of course, a delicious wine-inspired meal to accompany the fruits of the harvest. I've given this party many times, but I found out just how much people love it when I presented it on the *Today* show a couple years ago with Kathie Lee and Hoda—it quickly became their favorite party segment. (It has also been the highest rated video on my website to date.)

You don't have to be a wine connoisseur to enjoy this party, just an enthusiast. I suggest setting up a wine-tasting table with a wide selection of wines from all parts of the world. Whites should include Chardonnay, Sauvignon Blanc, and a Prosecco; reds can include a Chianti Classico, a Pinot Noir, and a Burgundy (see Styling Secrets, page 144) to add to the fun. The real enjoyment of this party is in the appreciation of good food, good friends, and good wine.

Because we have a house in Italy, wine has become an important part of our meals. Europeans nibble little bites as they drink wine, and that's the inspiration for this menu. Since the wine is the star of this party, I've surrounded it with simple dishes that are delicious and easy to prepare. This allows you to focus on your guests and participate in the wine talk. Both of the hot dishes can be prepared ahead of time, so there's not a lot of cooking to do on the day of the party.

Consider this a casual, kitchen-table party and don't sweat a lot of table decoration. If you have a rustic wooden dining table, you don't need to cover it with a white tablecloth—the look is reminiscent of a vineyard tasting table. If the fall weather is mild where you live, this can be a great outdoor party in the evening, always with lots of candles to illuminate the space.

If you want to combine this party with the Sunday Supper menu (page 149), you'll have a great menu with appetizers, wine, and a seated dinner. Of all the parties in the book, this one is the easiest. Have it anytime you think wine is appropriate and don't even wait for fall!

menu

Charcuterie Platter with Homemade Pickles

Pickled Red Onions

Sweet Pickles

Sweet Pepper Jam

Beet and Goat Cheese Salad with Thyme-Lime Dressing

White Bean and Tuscan Kale Soup with Broken Pasta

Apple, Pear, and Dried Fig Whole Wheat Cobbler

CHARCUTERIE PLATTER

with Homemade Pickles

Charcuterie—a selection of cured meats and sausages (available at delicatessens and most grocery stores) is a delicious accompaniment to the variety of wines you will be serving. Pair purchased salamis and hams—like prosciutto—with an assortment of cheeses and these homemade "quick" pickles and jams that guests can serve themselves. I love to serve the jams and pickles right out of their Mason jars, or in cool little bowls with antique forks or wooden serving spoons.

8 ounces prosciutto, thinly sliced

8 ounces Italian salami, such as Genoa salami, sliced

Assortment of cheeses, including 1 (4-ounce) wedge Parmesan and 1 (4-ounce) wedge goat cheese

2 cups assorted olives, such as Kalamata, Cerignola, and Picholine

1 (12-ounce) jar Pickled Red Onions (see recipe opposite)

1 (24-ounce) jar Sweet Pickles (see recipe opposite)

1 (24-ounce) jar Sweet Pepper Jam (see recipe opposite)

1 jar quince spread (store-bought and served in the jar)

French baguette, sliced 1 inch thick

Use various platters and cutting boards, mixing marble, wood, and slate. Place all the meats and cheeses on the platter or cutting boards.

Put the olives, pickled onions, sweet pickles, pepper jam, and quince spread in jars and small bowls and gather them beside the charcuterie arrangement. Place the bread in a bag or on a platter nearby.

Encourage guests to eat the cheese and jams with the bread, and pair the pickles with the charcuterie.

PICKLED RED ONIONS

Makes 1 (12-ounce) jar

Pickling vegetables is a great way to enhance their flavors. Great with meats and cheeses, as part of the appetizer or main course, pickles can add extra layers of flavor to your meals. These quick-pickled onions are not meant to be stored for long periods—eat them within two weeks.

1 large red onion, thinly sliced

1 cup red wine vinegar

3 tablespoons sugar

2 tablespoons salt

1 teaspoon celery seed

Combine all the ingredients with 1/2 cup water in a medium saucepan and bring to a boil over high heat. Continue to boil for 1 minute, then remove from the heat and let the onion mixture steep, uncovered, until it cools to room temperature.

Pour the pickles and the liquid into a Mason jar, cover tightly, and refrigerate for 2 days before using. These pickles can be kept, refrigerated, for 2 weeks.

SWEET PICKLES

Makes 1 (24-ounce) jar

5 small pickling or Persian cucumbers, sliced into coins

2 cups red wine vinegar

6 tablespoons sugar

1/4 cup salt

2 teaspoons celery seed

8 whole cloves

Combine all the ingredients with 1 cup water in a medium saucepan. Bring to a boil over high heat. Continue to boil for 1 minute, then remove from the heat and let the cucumbers steep, uncovered, until

they have cooled to room temperature. Pour the pickles and the liquid into a Mason jar, cover tightly, and refrigerate for 2 days before using. These pickles can be kept, refrigerated, for 2 weeks.

SWEET PEPPER JAM

Makes 1 (24-ounce) jar

6 cups chopped and seeded red bell peppers

2 garlic cloves, peeled

2 teaspoons crushed red pepper flakes

1/2 cup white vinegar

1/2 cup sugar

1 tablespoon unsalted butter

1/2 teaspoon salt

In the bowl of a food processor, pulse the peppers, garlic, and red pepper flakes for 10 to 20 seconds, until the mixture is pureed.

In a large saucepan over high heat, stir together the vinegar, sugar, butter, and salt. Stir in the pepper puree and bring to a boil. Boil the pepper jam for 1 minute, then remove from the heat and let cool to room temperature in the pan. Transfer to a glass or Mason jar, cover tightly, and chill in the refrigerator for 2 days before using. The pepper jam can be kept, refrigerated, for 1 week.

Use a wooden letter from the craft store and tie your initial onto the stack of napkins to create an instant monogram detail.

BEET AND GOAT CHEESE SALAD

with Thyme-Lime Dressing

Serves 6 to 8

I like to serve the beet salad on individual salad plates with tiny glass beakers of dressing on the side. Serving the dressing in individual portions allows guests to dress their salad as they wish. It also prevents overdressing the salad, which can ruin the flavors of the vegetables in this recipe.

SALAD

6 large red beets, scrubbed
6 cups arugula
1/2 cup soft fresh goat cheese

DRESSING

1/4 cup lime olive oil (see Source Guide, page 222)
1/4 cup fresh lime juice
1/4 cup plain Greek-style yogurt
3 tablespoons finely chopped shallot
3 tablespoons fresh thyme leaves
1 teaspoon grated lime zest

Preheat the oven to 350° F.

In a shallow baking pan, roast the beets in their skin for 45 minutes. Allow the beets to cool, then peel and slice them into 1/2-inch coins. Note: To avoid staining your hands, use gloves or a knife and fork to hold the beets in place while you peel them.

To make the dressing, place all the dressing ingredients in a container or jar with a lid and shake until well combined.

Divide the arugula among small individual plates and arrange the beets atop the greens. Dollop with teaspoons of goat cheese, then serve the dressing on the side in individual portions.

WHITE BEAN AND KALE SOUP

with Broken Pasta

Serves 6 to 8

Soup is a great party food. That's surprising, isn't it? But it shouldn't be; soup is a delicious, nutritious way to feed a lot of people. Having the soup ready on your cooktop while guests mingle and chat means you can relax and enjoy your own party sooner. Invite guests to serve themselves when they are ready, and they will appreciate the freedom—this works especially well at a wine-tasting party. All you need are soup mugs and spoons and you are ready to go. This soup is a great weekday meal for family, too.

1/4 cup olive oil
2 celery ribs, diced
1/2 yellow onion, coarsely chopped
2 garlic cloves, minced
4 bunches kale, stems and ribs removed and leaves chopped (about 8 cups)
2 carrots, cut into coins
1 cup chopped fresh Italian parsley
8 cups chicken stock
1 (14-ounce) can cannellini beans, with liquid
8 ounces spaghetti, broken into 3-inch pieces
2 cups grated Parmesan cheese, for serving
Extra virgin olive oil, for serving

Heat the oil in a large stockpot over medium heat. Add the celery, onion, and garlic and sauté for 3 minutes, or until the onion is translucent. Add the kale, carrots, and parsley. Pour in the chicken stock and bring to a simmer, then reduce the heat to low. Continue to simmer for 1 hour, then add the cannellini beans and their liquid. Simmer, covered, over low heat for 3 hours, or until creamy.

Ten minutes before you are ready to serve, add the broken pasta, and continue to simmer until the pasta is al dente.

Let guests serve themselves and have a bowl of the grated Parmesan and extra virgin olive oil nearby for guests to sprinkle on their soup.

Place the mugs, spoons, a bowl of shredded Parmesan cheese, and the bread near the soup pots.

How to make a
WINE CRATE CENTERPIECE

MATERIALS:

Small plastic garbage bag
Small (12 x 13-inch) wooden wine crate
4 (3 x 12-inch) blocks oasis (a light porous
    material used as a base for flower
    arrangements, available at craft stores)
2 dozen fresh red roses
6 empty wine bottles
3 (6-inch) lengths of twine
6 (6-inch) slender taper candles (with
    1/2-inch-wide base)
Scissors

DIRECTIONS:

1. Place the garbage bag in the bottom of the wooden crate.

2. Soak the oasis blocks in water for 2 minutes, or until soaked through.

3. Center the oasis blocks on the plastic in the crate, leaving room for wine bottles on either side.

4. Trim the roses so that they reach 3 inches above the top of the box when inserted into the oasis. You will need to test how far you need to insert them to keep them upright. Insert the stems of the roses into the oasis to

make a bouquet that reaches 3 inches above the top of the box. Leave room in the box for wine bottles to be placed on either side of the roses in the box.

5. Place 3 empty wine bottles on each side of the roses.

6. Wrap a 6-inch length of twine around the neck of each bottle and tie in a knot or bow.

7. Securely place 1 candle into each bottle.

How to make a
MAGAZINE TABLE RUNNER

MATERIALS:

1 *Wine Spectator* magazine
3 rolls of washi tape (decorative Japanese
    masking tape) in different colors

DIRECTIONS:

1. Cut out pages with images of large wine bottles and grapes from the magazine.

2. Lay the pages down the middle of the table, slightly overlapping, the length of the table. Leave a 12-inch overhang on the end of each side of the table, creating a table runner.

3. Tape the pages together where they overlap, using washi tape in alternating colors.

Styling Secrets

USE LARGE SLABS OF STONE, WOOD, OR SLATE AS PLATTERS FOR THE CHARCUTERIE.

MAKE HANDWRITTEN SIGNS FOR THE TYPES OF MEATS, JAM, PICKLES, AND CHEESES, SO GUESTS KNOW WHAT THEY ARE TRYING.

TIE A STACK OF NAPKINS WITH STRING AND PLACE THEM NEXT TO THE UTENSIL CONTAINERS AND THE INDIVIDUAL SERVING BOWLS AND PLATES.

SET UP A WINE-TASTING TABLE WITH LOTS OF GLASSES AND OPEN BOTTLES OF WINE AND SIGNS TO SUGGEST PAIRINGS WITH DISHES ON YOUR MENU, INCLUDING A DESSERT

WINE. WRITE THE PAIRINGS ON A LARGE PIECE OF SLATE OR A BLACKBOARD.

APPLE, PEAR, AND DRIED FIG WHOLE WHEAT COBBLER

Serves 8

This is my version of an apple cobbler. Since it's not a dish that Italians know, I decided to cook a cobbler for my Italian friends one night when I was in Italy. Our home in Italy is surrounded by rosemary bushes, so I picked some for the apple cobbler. I chopped the leaves and tossed them in with the apples and figs and my Italian friends loved the taste. Since fresh figs are available in the summer, you can substitute 1 cup fresh sliced figs in place of the dried figs if you make this recipe in the summer months.

2 red apples, such as Red Delicious or Honeycrisp, peeled, cored, halved, and cut into 2-inch slices

2 Granny Smith apples, peeled, cored, halved, and cut into 2-inch slices

2 Bartlett pears, peeled, cored, halved, and cut into 2-inch slices

1/2 cup chopped dried figs

1 Meyer lemon, halved

1 1/2 cups plus 6 tablespoons sugar, divided

2 tablespoons cornstarch

1 teaspoon coarsely chopped fresh rosemary

1 1/2 teaspoons sea salt, divided

1 cup whole wheat flour

1 cup all-purpose flour

1 teaspoon baking powder

3/4 cup (1 1/2 sticks) unsalted butter, chilled, cut into cubes, plus extra for greasing the baking dish

3/4 cup plus 2 tablespoons buttermilk, divided

Vanilla ice cream or whipped cream, for serving

Preheat the oven to 375° F.

Butter a 2 1/2-quart (9 x 9-inch) baking dish.

Place the apples, pears, and figs in a large mixing bowl. Squeeze the lemon halves over the fruit.

Add 1 1/2 cups of the sugar, the cornstarch, rosemary, and 1/2 teaspoon of the salt and toss to combine. Set aside.

To prepare the biscuits, combine the whole wheat flour, all-purpose flour, 4 tablespoons of the remaining sugar, the baking powder, and the remaining 1 teaspoon sea salt in a medium mixing bowl. Use 2 forks, or your hands, to cut in the cold cubes of butter until the dough is the consistency of crumbs. Pour 3/4 cup of the buttermilk slowly into the dough, stirring as you pour, to form a soft dough ball.

Transfer the dough ball onto a floured surface and roll out to a thickness of 1/2 inch. Use a biscuit cutter to cut circular dough rounds. Re-roll any dough scraps you need to make a total of 12 dough rounds.

Place the fruit in the buttered baking dish. Cover the fruit with the biscuit rounds, overlapping them 1/2 inch to form a continuous cobbler crust. Brush the crust with the remaining 2 tablespoons buttermilk and dust with the remaining 2 tablespoons sugar. Bake for 1 hour to 1 hour and 15 minutes, until the crust browns. Remove from the oven and let the cobbler cool slightly before serving.

Serve the warm cobbler with vanilla ice cream or whipped cream on top.

How to make
OLIVE AND BREAD BAGS

MATERIALS:

2 small Kraft paper gift bags with handles
Stick-on black letters, your choice of styles
Small plastic bag to fit inside
Scissors

DIRECTIONS:

1. Cut 3 inches off the top of one of the gift bags, including the handles.

2. Fold the top of the bag down twice to form a 3-inch cuff on the top of the bag.

3. Use the stick-on letters to write "Olives" on the front of the bag.

4. Place the olives in a plastic bag small enough to fit inside the paper bag. Once the plastic bag of olives is inside the cuffed bag, add more olives until you fill the bag to the top, creating an abundant display of olives.

5. Repeat to make a "Bread" bag. Fill this bag generously with 1-inch-thick slices of a French baguette to create an abundant display.

ELEMENTS

SERVING PIECES
2 cake stands, for jams and cheeses
Pie server

PLATTERS + SERVING BOWLS
3 small bowls, for pickles and jams

GLASS
16 wine glasses
6 empty wine bottles, for centerpiece project
8 small bottles, for individual dressing portions

CERAMIC
24 small plates, for charcuterie, salad, and dessert
Square (9 x 9-inch) baking dish, for cobbler

METAL
2 small forks, for pickles
1 small spoon, for jam
2 forks, for charcuterie
8 each: forks, knives, soupspoons, and dessert forks
8 small mugs for soup

TEXTILES
8 napkins

PAPER + STRING
Twine, for bottles in centerpiece and napkins

CANDLES + ILLUMINATION
6 pillar candles

WOOD
2 wood cutting boards, for charcuterie
3 small wood cutting boards, for risers for
pickles and jams
Wine crate, for centerpiece
Small crate, for utensils

STONE
2 marble cutting boards, for cheeses and charcuterie
1 piece of slate, or a blackboard, for menu of
wines, with chalk to write with

FLOWERS
2 dozen fresh red roses

Sunday supper

If you are just starting to host your own dinner parties, this is a great one to start with. Sunday suppers are usually family gatherings, but are equally popular as a way to see friends at the end of the week. In many ways, I consider this the most important chapter in this book. I am a firm believer in gathering your family around the dinner table at least once a week—in fact, it's my mission in life. It makes for a tighter family bond, and smarter, happier children.

You don't need to worry too much about which glasses and plates to use because the point of this gathering is that it is comfortable and homey for your family and guests. Just having a few flowers on the table for a Sunday supper is enough to make it special. I've included a fun decorative idea and how-to for using a painted clay pot as a menu blackboard, something that you could use in other parties, too.

This party is all about comfort food that is easy to prepare. On the menu: everybody's favorite roast chicken, risotto, and broccoli rabe, and my husband's favorite cookies combined with ice cream to make chocolate-chip ice cream sandwiches. Use this menu as a starting pont for making Sunday suppers a delicious ritual in your home.

menu

Sun-Dried Tomato and Olive Bread

Porcini Mushroom Risotto

Hot Garlic Broccoli Rabe

My Roast Chicken

Homemade Chocolate Chip Ice Cream Sandwiches

SUN-DRIED TOMATO AND OLIVE BREAD

Makes 4 small loaves

I like quick breads. One year I became obsessed with baking breads of all kinds, and this recipe in particular stuck with me. It's easy to make and perfect for this comfort food meal. It's also a great bread to freeze, so I freeze a few loaves and use them as needed. Remember, bread makes wonderful hostess or holiday gifts, too.

2 tablespoons unsalted butter, softened

3 cups all-purpose flour, plus 2 tablespoons for the pans

2 teaspoons double-acting baking powder

1 teaspoon baking soda

1 teaspoon salt

2 tablespoons sugar

1/2 cup sun-dried tomatoes packed in oil, drained and chopped, plus 2 tablespoons oil from the jar

2 garlic cloves, minced

1 teaspoon crumbled dried rosemary

1 teaspoon freshly ground black pepper

2 large eggs

1 1/2 cups whole milk

3 tablespoons unsalted butter, melted and cooled to room temperature

1 cup chopped pitted Kalamata or other brine-cured black olives

1/2 cup minced fresh Italian parsley leaves

1 cup grated Parmesan cheese

Preheat the oven to 350° F.

Butter and flour 4 (5 3/4 x 3 1/4-inch) loaf pans. Into a large mixing bowl, sift together the flour, baking powder, baking soda, salt, and sugar. Set aside.

Heat the oil from the sun-dried tomatoes in a small skillet over medium-low heat and sauté the garlic with the rosemary and pepper for 3 to 5 minutes, stirring, until it is soft but not browned.

In a separate large bowl, whisk together the eggs, milk, and butter with the garlic mixture. Add the flour mixture and stir until the batter is just combined. Do not overmix. Stir in the sun-dried tomatoes, chopped olives, parsley, and Parmesan, then divide the batter among the 4 loaf pans and bake for 35 to 40 minutes, or until a knife placed into the center of the bread comes out clean.

Turn the breads out from the loaf pans and transfer them to a rack to cool. The breads will keep, wrapped in plastic and foil and refrigerated, for 1 week, or frozen for 1 month.

PORCINI MUSHROOM RISOTTO

Serves 6

This is my son's favorite risotto, and he is a self-professed risotto expert. He loves to make this recipe—in fact, it is one of the first things he learned to cook. It's always nice to see your children love what you love to do.

1 ounce dried porcini mushrooms

2 cups warm water

3 cups chicken stock

2 tablespoons olive oil

2 tablespoons butter, divided

2 shallots, chopped

1 1/2 cups Arborio rice

1/2 teaspoon salt

8 ounces (1 cup) grated Parmesan cheese

1/4 teaspoon pepper

Place the mushrooms in a bowl and cover with the 2 cups warm water. Let the mushrooms soak for 1 1/2 hours, or until reconstituted. When the mushrooms become spongy, use a fork to remove them from the water, then chop them and set aside. Reserve the mushroom soaking water.

Combine the 3 cups chicken stock and the 2 cups mushroom soaking water in a large saucepan and bring to a simmer over medium heat. Reduce the heat to low and cover.

In a large sauté pan, heat the oil with 1 tablespoon of the butter over medium heat. Add the shallots, rice, and salt. Stir well until the rice is well coated and cook for 4 minutes, or until the rice begins to sizzle. Ladle 1/2 cup of the warm stock into the rice, and continue to cook, stirring constantly, until the stock is absorbed. You will use all 5 cups of stock. Continue to add the stock, 1/2 cup at a time, stirring until it is absorbed, for 18 to 20 minutes, until the rice is creamy. Stir in the mushrooms, then add the Parmesan, the remaining 1 tablespoon butter, and the pepper, continuously stirring until the cheese and butter are melted. Remove the pan from the heat, cover, and allow to cool for 2 minutes, then stir again and serve immediately.

HOT GARLIC BROCCOLI RABE

Serves 6

If you've never cooked broccoli rabe, this is a great way to try it. And, if you prefer a traditional broccoli, this recipe works fine, too. Just substitute broccoli florets for the rabe.

3 tablespoons olive oil
2 garlic cloves, minced
3 bunches broccoli rabe, bottom 1 inch of the stems trimmed
1 teaspoon crushed red pepper flakes
1 teaspoon salt

In a large sauté pan over medium heat, heat the oil and sauté the garlic for 3 minutes, or until it is translucent. Add the broccoli rabe plus 1 teaspoon water. Cover and cook for 5 minutes, or until the broccoli rabe turns bright green. Remove the pan from the heat and allow the broccoli rabe to rest for 3 minutes in the pan, then sprinkle with the red pepper flakes and salt. Serve warm.

MY ROAST CHICKEN

Serves 6

It has been said that you can recognize a good cook by their roasted chicken. I learned to make this one from a chef friend. She always massaged the chicken with an herb mixture, and I think that's the key to this recipe—that, plus a very hot oven. The vegetables layered under the chicken in the roasting pan add great flavor to the pan drippings.

1 (4- to 5-pound) roaster chicken, preferably organic
1/4 cup olive oil
3 garlic cloves, minced
3 tablespoons chopped fresh rosemary
2 teaspoons coarse salt
4 lemons, halved
8 small carrots
1 medium red onion, quartered
2 apples, quartered

Preheat the oven to 400° F.

In a small mixing bowl, stir together the oil, garlic, rosemary, salt, and the juice of 2 of the lemon halves. Rub the mixture all over the chicken, place the lemon rinds in the cavity of the chicken, and tie the legs together with kitchen string.

In the bottom of a roasting pan, layer the carrots, onions, apples, and the remaining lemon halves. Place a roasting rack on top of the vegetables and place the dressed chicken on the rack.

Roast the chicken in the oven for 1 hour, or until a meat thermometer inserted into the center of the breast reads 150° F. Remove from the oven, cover the pan loosely with aluminum foil, and allow the chicken to rest for 10 minutes before carving and serving. Serve the roast vegetables on a platter with the chicken, spooning any pan drippings over the top.

How to make
CANDLE POTS

MATERIALS:

2 (4-inch) oasis balls, soaked in water for 1 minute
2 (4-inch) terra-cotta pots
1 bunch orange berry branches (you can buy these from a florist or an upscale grocery), or berry branches from the garden
2 (2-inch-diameter x 4-inch-high) pillar candles
Scissors

DIRECTIONS:

1. Place a water-soaked oasis into each terra-cotta pot.

2. Cut the berry branches into 3-inch lengths.

3. Stick the berry branches in the oasis, leaving a space in the top of each oasis open for the candle.

4. Push a candle into the middle of each oasis to secure it. The candle should be surrounded by the berry branches.

HOMEMADE CHOCOLATE CHIP ICE CREAM SANDWICHES

Makes 12

Wrap these yummy ice cream sandwiches in white parchment paper and tie them with red-and-white baker's twine. Not only does this look appealing, it also holds the sandwiches together in the freezer until they are cold enough to serve.

CHOCOLATE CHIP COOKIES

Makes 2 dozen cookies

2 cups all-purpose flour
1/2 cup whole wheat flour
1 teaspoon salt
1 teaspoon baking soda
3/4 cup sugar
3/4 cup packed brown sugar
1 cup (2 sticks) unsalted butter, softened
1 teaspoon vanilla extract
2 large eggs
1 (12-ounce) package semisweet chocolate morsels
1 cup chopped walnuts (optional)

Preheat the oven to 375° F.

Combine both flours, the salt, and baking soda in a medium mixing bowl.

In the bowl of a standing mixer fitted with a paddle, blend the sugars, butter, and vanilla for 3 to 5 minutes on medium speed until creamy. With the motor still running, add the eggs one at a time, then slowly add the flour mixture and pulse for 1 minute, or until well blended. Stir in the chocolate morsels and walnuts, if using.

On a parchment-lined cookie sheet, drop rounded tablespoonfuls (I sometimes use a 2-inch ice cream scoopful) of dough about 1 inch apart. Bake for 10 to 12 minutes, or until golden brown. Let the cookies cool completely before you remove them from the pan. Repeat the process until all the dough is used.

VANILLA ICE CREAM

Makes 6 cups

3 cups heavy cream
1 cup whole milk
1/2 cup sugar
1 teaspoon vanilla extract
6 large eggs plus 2 large egg yolks

In a large saucepan over medium heat, bring the cream, milk, sugar, and vanilla to a simmer, and continue to cook for 10 minutes, or until the milk is scalded, then remove from the heat.

Meanwhile, in a separate bowl, whisk the eggs and yolks until creamy. Whisk 1/4 cup of the hot milk mixture into the egg mixture. Pour the warm egg mixture back into the saucepan of hot milk, return it to medium heat, and simmer for 5 to 7 minutes, until the custard thickens enough to coat the back of a metal spoon. Refrigerate the custard for 1/2 to 1 hour. Put the custard into an electric ice cream maker and follow the manufacturer's instructions to make ice cream.

When the ice cream is ready, place 1 scoop of ice cream on the bottom of a cookie, cover the ice cream with another cookie to make a sandwich, and stand it sideways in a loaf pan lined with plastic wrap. Working quickly, repeat with the rest of the cookies until the ice cream sandwiches fill the loaf pan. Place the loaf pan in the freezer for 3 hours, or until the sandwiches have frozen solid.

Cut 12 (3- x 6-inch) pieces of parchment paper.

Remove the sandwiches from the loaf pan, wrap each one in parchment paper, and tie with baker's string. Return the sandwiches to the freezer until you are ready to serve.

> Wrap and freeze ice cream sandwiches in parchment for a great presentation. These are easy to make the day before.

Styling Secrets

WELCOME GUESTS WITH A CHALKBOARD MENU (SEE DIY PROJECT, PAGE 156) AS THE CENTERPIECE.

WRAP A LOAF OF BREAD WITH PAPER AND STRING TO ADD A PRETTY TOUCH.

USE AN OLD CAKE PAN OR BAKING DISH LINED WITH WHITE PARCHMENT TO SERVE HOMEMADE BREAD AND BUTTER.

USE METAL AND PEWTER PLATTERS AND BOWLS TO ADD A BIT OF RUSTIC CHIC TO YOUR SUNDAY SUPPER.

USE A CENTERPIECE AND CANDLES, BUT KEEP THEM SIMPLE. USE CLOTH NAPKINS AND A TABLECLOTH TO DRESS UP YOUR SUNDAY SUPPER.

How to make a
MENU VASE

MATERIALS:

Painter's tarp
1 (8-inch) terra-cotta pot
1 can chalkboard spray paint
Chalk
Glass vase, slightly shorter than the
    terra-cotta pot
3 dozen fresh mums or dahlias

DIRECTIONS:

1. Spread the tarp on a work surface in a well-ventilated space.

2. Spray the terra-cotta pot with the chalkboard paint, using 2 coats to cover, and allowing it to dry between coats.

3. Let the paint dry completely.

4. Write your menu on the pot with chalk.

5. Place a glass vase half-filled with water inside the menu pot.

6. Arrange the flowers in the glass vase and use the menu vase as the centerpiece of your table.

~MENU~
ROAST CHICKEN
MUSHROOM RISOTTO
BROCCOLI RABE
OLIVE BREAD
ICE CREAM SANDWICH

Thanksgiving Celebration

Bringing family together and giving thanks for all the blessings of the year makes this just about everyone's favorite holiday. I love the comforting flavors, the grand pomp of placing a turkey on the table, the tradition of serving everyone's favorite things—it's not often you can put a family meal on the table where everyone has the same food expectations.

Growing up in a family with immigrant parents, Thanksgiving was very important to us. Although my parents didn't really understand the origins of the celebration, they were proud to be Americans so they embraced this day. We didn't know how to cook traditional Thanksgiving dishes, so we would always go to American friends' homes for Thanksgiving, and that's how we came to love Thanksgiving food. My gourmet father fell in love with stuffing, as well as the turkey and its trimmings. I looked forward to Thanksgiving when I was a child because I got to eat marshmallows and pumpkin pie. What an exotic treat!

As an adult I learned to cook all the Thanksgiving specialties, and my children love them all as much as I did. The one holdout was my husband. His family was from Germany and he had always eaten red cabbage—a very German dish—for Thanksgiving. It took ten years of

marriage before I could remove the red cabbage from the menu and teach him to love American dishes.

The dishes in this chapter are all adapted from the recipes of my parents' friends who hosted us so many years ago. Two years ago, I roasted a capon instead of a turkey, and there was a full-scale revolt in our family. My husband was so upset that people in his office were sending him their e-mail condolences, concerned that I would serve it the next year, too. I didn't—but I'm not bringing back the red cabbage, either.

The beauty of this time of year is that you can bring so many natural elements to your table décor—sometimes straight from your own yard. You can decorate with fresh fruits and veggies, dried branches, gourds and nuts, and acorn pods. I like to use pumpkins as a decorative table element. Heirloom pumpkins come in all different shapes, sizes, and colors. And I love the dramatic contrast of a black tablecloth with the orange and gold squash—fall colors are not just for Halloween. All of these things can live in your house from the beginning of October to early December, so have fun with them and feel free to use your favorite color combination—whatever it may be—on your table.

menu

The Ginger Snap Cocktail

Acorn Squash Soup with Sage Croutons

Roast Turkey with Pear, Walnut, and Bacon Stuffing

Kumquat Cranberry Sauce

Green Beans with Crispy Shallots and Mushrooms

Pumpkin Bread Pudding

THE GINGER SNAP COCKTAIL

Makes 8 cocktails

Serve a signature cocktail as guests arrive—it's a great way to start any holiday. I like to set up a bar with the cocktail premixed in a glass pitcher, and the glasses already filled with ice, a sprig of rosemary, and the flamed orange peel for guests to help themselves. Placing an arrangement of fall color flowers like marigolds and branches adds a nice touch of autumn to the décor.

Juice of 4 oranges
8 ounces (1 cup) Cointreau liqueur
16 ounces Snap organic liqueur, a ginger snap
　flavored liqueur (see Source Guide, page 222)
1 cup ginger ale
10 cups ice
8 thin slices orange peel
8 fresh rosemary sprigs

Fill a glass pitcher with the orange juice, add the Grand Marnier, and then the Snap liqueur. Top with a splash of ginger ale, add 2 cups of ice, and stir.

Flame the orange rind, rub the peel around the rims of the glasses, and drop it into the glasses. Garnish with a sprig of rosemary. Note: Flame the peels and place them in the glasses before the party starts.

To flame the orange rind, cut a 1- to 2-inch strip of orange peel. Light a match and hold it several inches above the cocktail. Hold the orange peel beside the match (not above), about 1 inch from the flame, then twist and squeeze the peel to bring the oil to the surface of the rind. It should flame a bit from the mist of oil. Rub the caramelized peel around the rim of the glass and drop it into the drink.

ACORN SQUASH SOUP

with Sage Croutons

Serves 8

I like to start our Thanksgiving meal with this warm, rich soup. It's a great soup to make throughout the fall and winter. Buy extra acorn squash and use them for your table decoration.

3 acorn squash, halved, seeds removed
1/2 cup olive oil, divided, plus 2 tablespoons for
　serving
2 teaspoons salt, divided
1 teaspoon pepper
2 Granny Smith apples, peeled, cored, and chopped
1 medium shallot, diced
1/2 yellow onion, diced
1 cup diced celery
1 teaspoon chopped fresh sage
1 teaspoon ground ginger
1/4 teaspoon ground cinnamon
4 cups vegetable stock, plus 1 cup to thin the
　soup as desired
Sage Croutons (see recipe opposite)

Preheat the oven to 400° F. Line a baking sheet with parchment paper.

In a large mixing bowl, toss the squash halves with 1/4 cup of the olive oil, 1 teaspoon of the salt, and the pepper. Place the squash, cut-side up, on the prepared baking sheet and roast for 45 to 50 minutes, or until the squash is tender and the skin begins to turn golden brown. Remove from the oven and set aside to cool on the pan.

Once cooled, use a spoon to scoop out the flesh of the squash and transfer to a bowl.

Heat the remaining 1/4 cup olive oil in a heavy large pot over medium-high heat, add the apples, shallot, onion, and celery, and sauté for 6 to 8 minutes, until tender. Add the remaining 1 teaspoon salt, the sage, ginger, cinnamon, cooked squash, and 4 cups vegetable stock and stir to combine.

Increase the heat to high and bring to a boil. Continue to boil for 5 minutes, then reduce the heat to low and simmer for 15 to 20 minutes. Remove the soup from the heat and let cool for 1 hour.

Ladle the soup in batches into a food processor and pulse for 30 seconds, or until smooth.

Place each batch into a large lidded container. The soup may be made 2 days before the party and refrigerated until ready to reheat.

Garnish with 2 tablespoons olive oil spooned onto the surface of the soup. You may use extra chicken stock to thin the soup if desired. Place in a large soup tureen with a stack of bowls with a bowl of sage croutons on the side and let guests help themselves.

Sage Croutons

Makes 3 cups

This recipe makes more than you will need. Leftovers can be stored in a sealed container in your pantry, or you can make great homemade breadcrumbs by crumbling the croutons into a food processor and processing them for 1 minute.

1/4 cup olive oil
2 garlic cloves, minced
1/4 cup chopped fresh sage
1/2 teaspoon sea salt
1/2 teaspoon pepper
1 loaf rustic bread, cut into 1-inch cubes

Preheat the oven to 350° F.

In a large mixing bowl, whisk together the oil, garlic, sage, salt, and pepper. Add the bread cubes and toss with the sage oil mixture to coat.

Transfer the coated bread cubes to a baking sheet and bake for 10 to 15 minutes, until golden brown. After 5 minutes, shake the baking sheet to toast the cubes evenly. Remove the croutons from the oven and set aside to cool. Seal in a zip-top plastic bag and keep until ready to serve.

Put place cards with names at each place setting; it makes it easier for your guests. I like to use very simple holders. A fun way to get the kids involved in the festivities is to have them write the names on the place cards and place them on the table. They can even get crafty and decorate them with leaves and berries.

ROAST TURKEY

with Pear, Walnut, and Bacon Stuffing

Serves 8

I like using an organic turkey. Not only is it healthier for you, it tastes better and is prepared the same way as a conventional turkey.

1 carrot, diced
2 celery ribs, diced
1 yellow onion, diced
2 cups turkey stock
1 (20-pound) organic turkey
1/4 cup olive oil
4 garlic cloves, minced
1/4 cup chopped fresh rosemary
2 teaspoons flaky salt
1 lemon

Preheat the oven to 350° F.

Place the carrots, celery, onion, and stock in the bottom of a roasting pan. Place a rack over the vegetables in the roasting pan and put the turkey on the rack. In a small bowl, whisk together the olive oil, garlic, rosemary, and salt and rub the entire turkey with the mixture.

Place the whole lemon into the cavity of the turkey and construct an aluminum foil tent over the top of the turkey to keep the skin from burning.

Roast in the oven for 4 hours, basting with the juices every 30 minutes. Remove the tent for the last hour of baking. The turkey is done when an instant-read meat thermometer placed into the meatiest part of the thigh reads 150° F.

Allow the turkey to rest for 15 to 30 minutes before carving. Reserve the vegetables in the roasting pan for the gravy recipe (see below).

While the turkey is resting, place the stuffing in the oven.

Pear, Walnut, and Bacon Stuffing

I like to assemble the stuffing in the morning then place it in the oven while the turkey is resting, giving me time to make the gravy.

1 cup walnut halves
3 links Italian sausage, casings removed, crumbled
5 slices bacon
1 yellow onion, chopped
2 celery ribs, chopped
3 garlic cloves, minced
1/4 cup chopped fresh sage leaves
1/4 cup chopped fresh rosemary
3 pears, cored and cubed
1 loaf Italian country bread, cubed
3 cups turkey stock

Preheat the oven to 350° F.

Toast the walnuts in a small skillet over medium heat for 3 to 5 minutes, until golden brown.

Sauté the crumbled sausage in a medium skillet over medium-high heat for 3 to 5 minutes, until the meat browns, then set aside.

In a large sauté pan over medium-high heat, cook the bacon until crispy, then drain on paper towels and set aside.

Using 1/4 cup of the bacon drippings left in the pan (discard the rest), sauté the onion, celery, and garlic for 5 minutes, or until the onions are translucent. Add the cooked sausage, the sage, rosemary, toasted walnuts, and pears, stir for 2 minutes, then remove the pan from the heat.

In a large bowl, combine the bread cubes and turkey stock, and add the sausage mixture from the sauté pan. Crumble the bacon into the bowl and mix the stuffing well using your hands.

Pour the stuffing into a 15 x 10-inch casserole dish. Bake for 30 minutes and serve warm.

Roasted Vegetable Gravy

Reserved roasted vegetables from roast turkey (see opposite)
2 cups turkey stock
2 tablespoons cornstarch

Pour the reserved roasted vegetables into a large saucepan over medium heat and remove any fat from the top layer. Add the turkey stock and continue to cook for 2 minutes, or until warm.

In a small bowl, combine the cornstarch with 3 tablespoons of the warm roasted vegetable broth and stir with a small spoon until a paste forms. Add the paste to the hot liquid in the saucepan and cook, stirring, for 5 to 7 minutes, until the gravy thickens.

Remove from the heat and strain the gravy into a bowl. Serve on the side with the turkey and stuffing.

KUMQUAT CRANBERRY SAUCE

Makes 4 cups

I love the combination of the tangy kumquats and the sweet-tart cranberries. It's the perfect complement to a roast turkey. This is best made a day ahead and chilled before serving—I like to serve it cold.

8 cups fresh cranberries
8 kumquats, sliced and seeded, or substitute
   1 chopped tangerine or clementine
1 cup fresh orange juice
1/2 cup sugar

Combine all the ingredients in a large saucepan over medium heat and cook for 10 minutes, or until the cranberries pop and the liquid has reduced. Remove from the heat and let cool. Cover and chill in the refrigerator for 1 day before serving.

Thanksgiving Takeaways

It's always a nice gesture to give guests a few leftovers, especially at Thanksgiving.

When dinner is finished, pack disposable containers with individual portions of your leftovers. Tuck the containers into a fabric bag—I like to use burlap bags—and attach a gift tag that says, "Loved having you."

I always stack these takeaway gifts where guests can grab them on the way out the door. For a lovely presentation, put a simple handwritten sign near them that says, "Please Take Home Leftovers."

GREEN BEANS

with Crispy Shallots and Mushrooms

Serves 8

1/4 cup plus 3 tablespoons olive oil, divided
3 shallots, thinly sliced
1 1/2 pounds haricot vert (green) beans, washed
   and trimmed
8 ounces brown mushrooms, sliced
1 teaspoon salt

Heat 1/4 cup of the olive oil in a large sauté pan over medium-high heat. Add the shallots and fry for 5 to 7 minutes, until crispy, then drain on paper towels.

Fill a large stockpot halfway with water and salt the water generously. Bring to a boil over high heat.

Fill a large bowl with ice water.

Add the green beans to the boiling water and cook for 2 minutes, or until the beans turn bright green and are tender but crisp. Drain the beans and transfer immediately to the bowl of ice water to stop the cooking. Drain and set aside.

Heat the remaining 3 tablespoons olive oil in a large sauté pan over medium heat. Add the mushrooms and salt and sauté for 4 minutes, or until browned. Add the blanched beans to the mushrooms and continue to sauté for 3 to 5 minutes, stirring, until the beans are softened.

Transfer the beans and mushrooms to a platter, sprinkle with the crispy shallots, and serve immediately.

PUMPKIN BREAD PUDDING

Serves 8

Although I love pumpkin pie, I realized that my husband loves bread pudding more, so this turns out to be a great marriage of the two desserts. This can be assembled before your meal and popped in the oven when you sit down for dinner. I like to assemble it in the afternoon while my turkey is in the oven.

6 large eggs
1 cup heavy cream, or substitute whole milk
3/4 cup canned organic pumpkin
1/2 cup sugar
1/2 teaspoon salt
1/2 teaspoon ground cinnamon
1/4 teaspoon ground nutmeg
1/8 teaspoon ground cloves
1/4 cup toasted walnuts, chopped
1 (20-inch) loaf day-old raisin bread, cut into 6
   cups of 1-inch cubes (I like to use raisin bread
   from my favorite bakery)
1/2 cup (1 stick) unsalted butter, melted
Vanilla ice cream or whipped cream, for serving

Preheat the oven to 350° F.

In a large mixing bowl, whisk together the eggs, cream, pumpkin, sugar, salt, cinnamon, nutmeg, and cloves. Stir in the walnuts.

In a separate large mixing bowl, toss the bread cubes with the melted butter. Add the pumpkin mixture and toss to coat the bread cubes. Transfer to an ungreased, 8-inch-square baking dish and bake for 25 to 30 minutes, until the custard is set and solid to the touch.

Serve warm with a dollop of vanilla ice cream or whipped cream.

Place individual servings of the pumpkin bread pudding on a sideboard with a coffee service and serve the ice cream or whipped cream in a separate chilled bowl so that guests can serve themselves.

How to make
BRANCH VOTIVES

MATERIALS:

2 (8- to 10-inch-tall, 4- to 5-inch-diameter)
  glass vases
12 (2- to 3-feet-long) bare branches
3 yards yarn in a natural or neutral color
2 votive candles
Garden clippers
Scissors

DIRECTIONS:

1. Clip the branches in uneven lengths,
but long enough to reach above the lip of
the vase when you stand them up in it.

2. Stand the branches side-by-side
around the vase to cover it and tie a
length of yarn around the branches to
hold them in place on the vase.

3. Wrap more yarn around the vase a few
times to neatly cover the original knot.

Tuck in the end of the yarn to hold in
place. Repeat to make another votive
holder.

4. Place a votive candle into the bottom
of each vase and light.

How to make a
CAKESTAND CORNUCOPIA

MATERIALS:

Large ceramic bowl, 10- to 12-inch
  diameter with 4- to 5-inch-high sides
1 cake stand, to fit into the ceramic bowl
4 each: apples, pears, gourds or acorn
  squash, and small pumpkins
1 pound red grapes
4 dried lotus pods

DIRECTIONS:

1. Place the bowl in the center of the dining table.

2. Place the cake stand into the center of
the bowl.

3. Arrange the apples, pears, and gourds
on the cake stand, leaving a few for the
bowl.

4. Put the grapes in the bowl and drape
them over the side.

5. Place 1 small pumpkin in the arrangement, either on the cake stand or in the
bowl. Place the other 3 pumpkins on the
table around the centerpiece.

6. Fill the empty spaces in the arrangement with the dried pods.

How to make a
NAPKIN EMBELLISHMENT

MATERIALS:

8 orange cloth napkins
8 burlap roses (see Source Guide,
  page 222)
3 yards yarn in a natural or neutral color
Scissors

DIRECTIONS:

1. Fold each napkin in half, then roll into a
loose tube.

2. Place a burlap
rose on top of the roll
and wrap a 1-foot
length of yarn twice
around the napkin
and tie in a bow over
the center of the rose.
Repeat for the rest of
the napkins.

3. Cut the ends of
the yarn to an even
length and place a
napkin on the center
of each plate.

ELEMENTS

SERVING PIECES
8 each: dinner plates, soup bowls, dessert bowls
8 cups and saucers
Fancy roaster, or platter, for turkey
2 casseroles: 1 for dressing and 1 for bread pudding
Medium bowl, for cranberry sauce
Square dish, for beans

GLASS
8 water glasses
8 highball glasses, for cocktails
1 glass pitcher, for signature cocktail
2 (4-inch-diameter) glass vases, for votive project
1 (12-inch-tall) vase, for flowers on the bar

METAL
8 each: forks, knives, spoons, and dessert forks
3 serving spoons
1 carving set, knife and fork, for turkey
8 place card holders

TEXTILES
8 orange cloth napkins
1 dark tablecloth
8 burlap bags, for takeaway packages
1 burlap runner
8 burlap roses

FLOWERS + FRUIT + VEGETABLES
4 gourds or acorn squash
4 small pumpkins
1 pound red grapes
4 apples
4 pears
4 dried pods
2 bunches marigolds, or any type orange
flowers for the bar

CERAMIC
1 pitcher for water
1 gravy boat
Bowl and cake stand for centerpiece

WOOD
Branches

PAPER + STRING
Yarn for candle votive project and napkins
Gift tags for leftover to-go packages
Place cards

Holiday Cocktail Open House

I call the weeks after Thanksgiving the fast slide into the New Year. Too much is always going on in everyone's lives to plan an intricate dinner party. Instead, this holiday open house is quick and easy to organize, with a lot of ready-made things on the menu to help you pull it off and still get your holiday shopping done. A cocktail open house is a great way to see your friends during this season, and you can even hold the party early in the evening so that your guests will have time to do some gift shopping, too. This open house can also be a template for a great office party.

As far as I'm concerned, the only rules for a holiday party are: 1) It must look festive, and 2) All the food and drinks should be easy to pick up and nibble. Break out the twinkly lights, glitter, and fake snow for this fête. The decorations and sparkly details make this a fun party for guests to bring their children. My mom always has a holiday open house, although hers is reserved for adults only. It's your choice, but I like to invite the children to this party.

Takeaway gifts are the most important things that you will plan and make ahead. I love easy DIY gift ideas, and the Truffled Popcorn is a perfectly easy take-home party favor that will wow your guests. (If kids are invited, plan to make an alternative popcorn takeaway using cinnamon and sugar. I have included both recipes.) Most of the recipes can be made ahead, too. Plus, you can use the DIY projects to decorate your own house after the party.

Last but not least, don't forget to break out the holiday playlist. I like a little holiday soul at my party—don't you?

menu

Candy Cane Martini

Limoncello Sangria

Caprese Salad Poppers with Basil Cream

The Stand Up Salad

Lemony Risotto Shrimp "Cocktails"
with Tomato Sauce

Roast Beef with Red Pepper Aioli in Pita Bread

Truffled Popcorn

Salty-Sweet Popcorn

Mini Crêpes with Nutella

Mini Pavlovas with Strawberry Sauce

CANDY CANE MARTINI

Serves 8

20 ounces (2½ cups) cranberry juice
16 ounces (2 cups) strawberry-flavored vodka
4 ounces (½ cup) white crème de menthe
8 mini candy canes, for garnish

In a large pitcher, stir together the cranberry juice, vodka, and crème de menthe. Chill in the refrigerator until cold; keep chilled until ready to serve.

Just before the party, place martini glasses in the refrigerator to chill.

Remove the pitcher from the refrigerator, stir again, then pour into chilled glasses and serve with a candy cane to garnish.

LIMONCELLO SANGRIA

Serves 8

This is another great pitcher drink that you can make ahead. You simply soak the fruit in the limoncello overnight before your party, then stir in the wine and soda just before serving.

2 cups limoncello liqueur
1 pint fresh strawberries, hulled and sliced
1 small blood orange, thinly sliced and quartered
1 cup seedless white grapes, halved
8 cups Sauvignon Blanc wine, chilled
3½ cups club soda, chilled

Macerate the fruit in the limoncello overnight, refrigerated, in a large pitcher.

When you are ready to serve, add the white wine and club soda to the pitcher, stir, and serve in champagne coupes.

CAPRESE SALAD POPPERS

with Basil Cream

Makes 24

I learned to make this appetizer at the Culinary Institute of America. I'm a sucker for creative presentation and this one, which incorporates serving tricks from molecular gastronomy, is really fun and festive and guests love it. First, you skewer cherry tomatoes and fresh mozzarella balls onto a pipette filled with a basil cream sauce. When serving, tell guests that the idea is to place the tomato and mozzarella in your mouth as you squeeze the pipette bulb to release the sauce in your mouth.

½ cup loosely packed fresh basil leaves
¼ cup loosely packed fresh Italian parsley leaves
½ cup mayonnaise
1 small garlic clove, peeled
1 teaspoon grated lemon zest
½ cup heavy cream
Salt and pepper
12 cherry tomatoes, halved
12 small balls fresh mozzarella (bocconcini), halved
24 (6-inch) pipettes, available online (see Source Guide, page 222)

Blanch the basil and parsley in a small pan of boiling water for 15 seconds. Remove and shock the herbs in ice water, then drain on paper towels.

Place the mayonnaise in the bowl of a food processor fitted with a blade. Grate the garlic into the mayonnaise using a fine grater or zester, then add the lemon zest and herbs. Process for 20 seconds, or until the herbs are finely minced. Add the cream and salt and pepper to taste, and process for 15 seconds. Set aside.

On the stem of each pipette, skewer a tomato half, and then a mozzarella half. Dip the end of the pipette into the bowl of basil cream and squeeze the bulb, drawing the cream into the bulb of the pipette. Using kitchen shears, clip 3 inches off the end of the pipette and place the completed "poppers" on a tray to serve.

Instruct guests to bite the tomato and cheese off the stem while simultaneously squeezing basil cream into their mouths.

Styling Secrets

DRAPE A STRING OF LIGHTS DIRECTLY ON THE BUFFET TABLE FOR INSTANT GLITTER AND SHINE.	PREPARE A PITCHER OF COCKTAILS 1 HOUR AHEAD OF TIME AND FREEZE OR REFRIGERATE UNTIL JUST BEFORE YOUR PARTY TO SAVE TIME.	AN OPEN HOUSE BUFFET IS ALL ABOUT INDIVIDUAL SERVINGS; THE NICEST WAY TO PRESENT ALL THE DIFFERENT NIBBLES IS GROUPED TOGETHER ON LOTS OF PRETTY TRAYS AND PLATTERS.	EVERYTHING ON THE BUFFET CAN BE EATEN WHILE STANDING OR SITTING, WITH A FORK OR FINGERS.	ARRANGE COCKTAILS ON A SILVER TRAY AND SERVE THEM TO GUESTS AS THEY ENTER THE PARTY.

Plastic pipettes are a super fun way to serve a deconstructed caprese salad. The basil cream–filled pipette is not only a conversation piece but it gives guests a playful appetizer to experience. The pop of flavor is sure to be a crowd-pleaser.

THE STAND UP SALAD

Serves 8

I love the idea of eating salad from a stemmed glass, or from a small bowl, at a cocktail party. I sometimes serve this salad before a sit-down meal, so guests can mingle and enjoy salad and a glass of wine as a prelude to a long dinner. There's no need to use matching glasses; just make sure they are all clear glass, with no etching or pattern on them.

1 small bunch watercress
1 cup roasted red peppers from a jar, cut into
   1/2-inch squares
1 small head radicchio, cut into strips
1 cup sun-dried tomatoes in oil, cut into
   1/2-inch squares
2 cups baby arugula
1 cup shredded Parmesan cheese

DRESSING
1/4 cup olive oil
1/4 cup balsamic vinegar
1/2 teaspoon salt
1/2 teaspoon pepper
1 small shallot, finely diced
1 tablespoon Dijon mustard

Line up the watercress, red peppers, radicchio, sun-dried tomatoes, arugula, and shredded Parmesan in separate bowls to assemble the individual salads.

In each of 8 serving glasses, build layers of ingredients, starting with enough watercress to fill one-sixth of the jar. Then add each of the ingredients, in this order: red peppers, radicchio, sun-dried tomatoes, arugula, and shredded Parmesan.

Whisk all the dressing ingredients together in a small bowl. Drizzle 4 teaspoonfuls of dressing onto each salad just before serving.

LEMONY RISOTTO SHRIMP "COCKTAILS"

with Tomato Sauce

Serves 8

Served in stemmed drinking glasses, this is really a full entrée that you can eat standing up, making it the perfect dish for any cocktail party. If you serve this at a seated dinner party, just pass the risotto and the shrimp in separate bowls. This should be the last thing you make on your party menu, and it can be assembled just before guests arrive. I like to use a small spoon to assemble each serving, carefully placing all the components into the drinking glass, then draping shrimp around the rim.

TOMATO SAUCE
3 tablespoons olive oil
3 large ripe tomatoes
3 garlic cloves, peeled
1/4 cup chicken stock

RISOTTO
4 cups chicken stock or canned low-salt
   chicken broth
1/4 cup lemon-flavored olive oil, preferably
   O. & Co. (see Source Guide, page 222)
4 tablespoons butter, divided in half
1 large shallot, chopped
2 cups Arborio rice or medium-grain white rice
1 cup freshly grated Parmesan cheese
2 tablespoons fresh thyme leaves
2 tablespoons fresh lemon juice
4 teaspoons grated lemon zest
1 teaspoon salt
1/2 teaspopn pepper

SHRIMP
2 tablespoons olive oil
2 pounds large shrimp, cleaned, tails left on
1/2 teaspoon salt

For the sauce: Heat the oil in a medium sauté pan over low heat, then add the tomatoes and garlic and sweat them for 1 1/2 hours, or until the tomatoes are mushy and caramelized. Mash with a fork in the pan, add the chicken broth to thin the sauce, and turn the heat to medium.

Cook for 2 minutes, then transfer the sauce to a serving bowl, leaving 2 tablespoons sauce in the sauté pan to cook with the shrimp.

For the risotto: Combine the 4 cups chicken stock with 2 cups water in a large saucepan and bring to a simmer over medium heat. Reduce the heat to low and cover to keep warm. Heat the lemon oil in a large sauté pan over medium heat and add 2 tablespoons of the butter.

When the butter has melted, add the shallot and rice. Cook for 4 minutes, stirring, until the rice is well coated and begins to sizzle.

Ladle 1/2 cup of the warm stock into the pan and stir constantly until it is absorbed. Continue to add the warm stock, 1/2 cup at a time, stirring constantly until each addition is absorbed and you have used all the stock, for 18 to 20 minutes, until the rice is al dente and the risotto is creamy. Stir in the Parmesan cheese and the remaining 2 tablespoons butter. Add the thyme, lemon juice, and lemon zest. Season with the salt and pepper, then remove from the heat, cover, and let stand while you prepare the shrimp.

For the shrimp: Heat the oil in the same sauté pan in which you cooked the tomato sauce with the reserved 2 tablespoons sauce in the pan, over medium

heat. Add the shrimp in 4 batches and sauté until they turn pink, then sprinkle with the salt, remove them from the heat, and set aside to assemble the mock cocktails. To assemble the individual servings, place 1 cup of risotto in each of 8 glasses, add 2 tablespoons sauce on top, then drape 4 shrimp around the rim of the glass. Arrange the filled glasses on a platter so that guests may serve themselves.

ROAST BEEF
with Red Pepper Aioli in Pita Bread

Serves 8 to 10

This is a super easy appetizer and the presentation is perfect for a holiday party. Use a good roast beef from a deli. Choose a decorative toothpick from your prop stash to secure the sandwiches, and line them up like little soldiers on a shiny platter.

1 garlic clove, peeled
1/2 teaspoon salt
1 egg yolk
2 teaspoons prepared red pepper pesto, your favorite brand
1/2 teaspoon Dijon mustard
1/4 cup olive oil
3 tablespoons vegetable oil
1 package mini pita pockets
1 pound rare roast beef, thinly sliced
1 small head butter lettuce, washed and separated into leaves
Decorative toothpicks, for securing

Mash the garlic clove and salt together with a fork to form a paste. Set aside.

In a medium mixing bowl, whisk together the egg yolk, red pepper pesto, and mustard.

In a separate bowl, mix the oils, then pour them into the yolk mixture in a steady stream, whisking constantly. If the aioli separates, add a little more oil and continue to whisk for 5 to 10 minutes, until it comes together. Whisk in the garlic paste and blend thoroughly. Cover and refrigerate until ready to use.

When you are ready to assemble the pitas, use a paring knife to slice a 2-inch opening on top of each mini pita and spread 1 tablespoon of the aioli inside. Stuff a folded slice of beef and a lettuce leaf inside each mini pita, and secure with a toothpick.

TRUFFLED POPCORN

Makes 8 cups

Make the popcorn the old-fashioned way for this recipe—it makes all the difference. You'll be surprised how good this popcorn tastes at room temperature. I like to place bowls of it around the room for guest to enjoy, plus it makes a great take-home gift for guests.

3 tablespoons canola oil
3/4 cup popping corn
1/4 cup white truffle oil, available at specialty stores such as Whole Foods or Williams-Sonoma
2 teaspoons truffle salt, available at specialty stores

Add the canola oil and 3 kernels of popping corn to a 6-quart stockpot over medium heat and cover. When you hear the kernels pop, remove the lid, add the remaining popcorn, and cook, covered, for 5 minutes, occasionally shaking the covered pan until the popping sounds stop.

Transfer the popcorn to a large serving bowl and toss with the truffle oil and salt. This popcorn is delicious served either warm or at room temperature.

SALTY-SWEET POPCORN

This is a sweet version for the kiddies. I like to fill take-home jars for the children—it's such a cute gift!

Makes 8 cups

6 tablespoons sugar
1 teaspoon ground cinnamon
1 1/2 teaspoons salt
3 tablespoons canola oil
3/4 cup popping corn
4 tablespoons melted butter

In a small bowl, stir together the sugar, cinnamon, and salt. Set aside.

Add the canola oil and 3 kernels of popping corn to a 6-quart stockpot over medium heat and cover. When you hear the kernels pop, remove the lid, add the remaining popcorn, and cook, covered, for 5 minutes, occasionally shaking the covered pan, until the popping sounds stop.

Transfer the popcorn to a large serving bowl and toss with the butter. Add the cinnamon sugar and salt to the bowl and stir to combine.

In a separate small bowl, stir together the cinnamon, sugar, and salt, then stir the mixture into the popcorn. This popcorn is delicious served either warm or at room temperature.

MINI CRÊPES

with Nutella

Makes 20 crêpes

This is a quick dessert that you can make just before the party. Everyone loves something chocolate, and using Nutella is a great way to serve a chocolate dessert with very little trouble.

1 cup all-purpose flour
1 cup whole milk
2 large eggs
2 tablespoons melted unsalted butter
Pinch of salt
1/4 cup vegetable oil
1 (13-ounce) jar Nutella chocolate-hazelnut spread
1/4 cup confectioners' sugar

In a medium mixing bowl, whisk together the flour, milk, eggs, melted butter, and salt. Using a pastry brush, coat a small crêpe pan with some of the oil and heat over medium heat. (I give the pan a fresh coating of oil after making each crêpe.) Spoon 2 tablespoons of the batter into the skillet, coating to form 3-inch-round crêpes. Make only one crêpe at a time. Cook for 1 minute, or until the crêpe bubbles, then turn and cook the other side for 1 minute, or until golden brown.

Stack the finished crêpes on an ovenproof plate, cover with aluminum foil, and place in a 200° F oven to keep warm. When you are ready to serve, place 1 teaspoon Nutella in the middle of each crêpe, fold the crêpe in half, and dust with confectioners' sugar. Serve immediately.

MINI PAVLOVAS

with Strawberry Sauce

Makes 18

Pavlovas are best prepared the morning of the event. These little poufs can sit at room temperature on the counter until you are ready to fill. When you are ready to serve, remove the paper liners and use a small spoon to carefully break open the tops. Fill each Pavlova with berries and sauce and serve on a pretty platter.

MERINGUE

1/4 cup cornstarch
1 tablespoon white vinegar
1 tablespoon vanilla extract
2 1/2 cups sugar
8 large egg whites, at room temperature

STRAWBERRY SAUCE

1 pint fresh strawberries
1 cup sugar

WHIPPED CREAM

1 cup heavy whipping cream
2 tablespoons sugar

ASSEMBLY

1 pint fresh strawberries, hulled and halved
Fresh mint sprigs, for garnish

For the meringue: Preheat the oven to 225° F. Place 18 paper baking cups on a baking sheet.

In a small bowl, stir together the cornstarch, vinegar, and vanilla and set aside.

In the bowl of a standing mixer with a whisk attachment, beat the sugar and egg whites on low speed until combined, then increase the speed to high and beat for 3 to 5 minutes, until soft peaks form. Add the cornstarch mixture and continue to beat for 2 minutes, or until the meringue is glossy. Fill a pastry bag fitted with a round tip with the meringue. Place the 18 paper baking cups on a cookie sheet and pipe each cup half full of the meringue. Bake for 45 minutes, then set the meringues aside to cool.

For the strawberry sauce: In a medium saucepan, combine the strawberries, sugar, and 1/4 cup water. Bring to a boil in a medium saucepan over medium heat and simmer for 10 minutes, or until the strawberries have cooked down. Strain the strawberries through a sieve into a bowl and use a rubber spatula to press on the strawberries, releasing more sauce into the bowl. Allow the sauce to cool to room temperature.

To assemble the pavlovas: Whip the cream with the 2 tablespoons sugar in the bowl of a standing mixer fitted with a whisk attachment for 3 to 5 minutes, or until soft peaks form. (Refrigerate covered until you are ready to assemble the desserts. The whipped cream can be made 3 hours ahead and refrigerated.)

To assemble the dessert: Use a small spoon to break a small opening in the top of each meringue. Pour 2 teaspoons of the strawberry sauce into the opening and add the strawberry halves and a dollop of the whipped cream, and garnish with a sprig of mint.

How to make
SNOW GLOBES

Place these on the buffet table for a festive alternative to flowers.

Makes 3 globes
(1 large, 1 medium, and 1 small)

MATERIALS:

1 of each: (4-inch, 23-inch, and 32-inch tall) bottle brush trees (see Source Guide, page 222)
1 each: (1- gallon, 2- quart, and 1- quart) screw-top cracker jars
3 (3½-ounce) packages loosely packed snow globe "snow," available at craft stores
Hot-glue gun

DIRECTIONS:

1. Warm the hot-glue gun and glue 1 bottle brush tree inside the lid of each jar lid, making certain that the bottle brush tree fits nicely inside the size appropriate jar.

2. Place 2 cups of snow into the jar.

3. When the glue is set, place the bottle brush tree into the jar by screwing the lid on the top of the jar, then invert the jar so that the lid forms the base of the globe.

4. Snow will cover the tree; shake to settle the snow.

How to make
ELFIN POPCORN JARS

Makes 8 takeaway gifts

MATERIALS:

8 (8-ounce) quilted Ball jars, with flat tops
8 elf ornaments (or substitute deer, angels, or snowflake ornaments), with a flat bottom to allow the glue to adhere
Scissors
Hot-glue gun
8 cups Truffled Popcorn (see recipe, page 178)

DIRECTIONS:

1. Plug the hot-glue gun in to warm, then place a small dot of hot glue on the bottom of an ornament and secure it to the top of one of the lids. Repeat with the remaining ornaments and lids and allow the glue to set.

2. When the glue is set, fill each jar with 1 cup of the popcorn, then screw an ornamented lid on each jar. Use these as little gifts for departing guests.

How to make a
HOLIDAY MESSAGE GARLAND

MATERIALS:

30 (4-inch) round paper disks, or as many
disks as you have letters in your greeting
(this banner says "eat drink and b merry")
6 (3-inch) round paper doilies, or as many
disks as you have letters in your greeting
(I only used 6 doilies)
1 sheet of (2-inch) stick-on letters
20-inch length of (3/4-inch-wide) red ribbon
Scissors
Hole punch
Glue, to stick the doilies to the disks

DIRECTIONS:

1. Punch 2 holes into the top of each disk,
about 1 1/2 inches apart.

2. Apply 1 letter to each disk to spell out
your greeting.

3. Use blank disks for the spaces between
words. Before you punch holes in these
blank disks, glue a lace doily to one side of
the disk. The lace detail will be the front of
the blank disk.

4. Lace the ribbon through the letters to
form your sentiment, starting and ending
with a blank disk.

5. Hang the garland over your buffet
table or in your home to greet guests.

comfort food get-together

When I first came up with the idea for this party, I didn't even think of it as a party—I just wanted to get together with some friends and make it a cozy, comfy, casual dinner. I was surprised that everyone I invited RSVPed (how often does that happen?), but I really shouldn't have been—in this hurried, digital world I think we're all hungry for the simple comforts of breaking bread (and it doesn't even have to be homemade) with our nearest and dearest. The party was such a success that since then I have one at least once a year and always invite close friends. It's become a treasured tradition and one of the parties I most enjoy hosting.

The beauty of this party is that it's easy to put together and it's sort of an all-occasion or no-occasion kind of deal. It's a great way to welcome new neighbors to the neighborhood, host a book club, or like I first did, just treat your friends with a little chicken soup—and white bean chili, and sausage and peppers, and grilled cheese sandwiches—for the body and soul. This is also a great "first party" if you're beginning to do some entertaining because its casual nature and simple, crowd-pleasing recipes yield amazing results.

The food is served on a buffet with soups and chili ladled right out of their pots on the stovetop. Plates and bowls are stacked and piled around so guests can mingle and serve themselves. Like the food, I keep the décor simple and homey, with rustic touches in subdued hues.

White Bean Vegetable Farro Soup
with Herby Chermoula

Roasted Chicken Noodle Soup

Grilled Cheese Sandwiches
with Brie, Crispy Bacon, and Apricot Jam

White Bean Chili

Sausage and Peppers for a Crowd

PB & J Thumbprint Cookies

Devil's Food Cupcakes

WHITE BEAN VEGETABLE FARRO SOUP

with Herby Chermoula

Serves 8

The chermoula is inspired by the delightful North African lemony, garlicky, herby marinade. This one is a great spicy herb sauce to use anytime with meat and fish. You can make it a day ahead and chill it, then bring to room temperature before serving.

CHERMOULA SAUCE

1 cup chopped fresh Italian parsley
1 cup chopped fresh cilantro
1 (2-inch) piece fresh ginger, peeled
3 garlic cloves, peeled
Juice of 1 lemon
1 cup olive oil
Salt and pepper
2 teaspoons coriander seeds

SOUP

1/4 cup olive oil
1 cup diced carrot
1/2 cup diced celery
1/2 medium onion, chopped
2 garlic cloves, minced
2 cups chopped kale
1 cup diced sweet potato
1 cup diced zucchini
1/2 cup chopped red bell pepper (optional)
8 cups vegetable stock
1 (15-ounce) can white beans, or 1 cup white beans
   that have been soaked overnight, then rinsed
2 tablespoons chopped fresh rosemary
2 tablespoons chopped fresh Italian parsley
1 cup farro
Salt and pepper

For the sauce: In the bowl of a food processor, combine all the ingredients and pulse for 1 minute, or until the mixture forms a loose, smooth sauce. The chermoula may be made a day ahead and refrigerated, covered, overnight.

For the soup: In a large stockpot, heat the oil over medium heat. Add the carrots, celery, onion, and garlic and sauté for 5 minutes, or until tender. Add the kale, sweet potato, zucchini, and red bell pepper (if using), and sauté for another 2 minutes. Add the vegetable stock, beans, rosemary, and 1/4 cup water as needed to thin the soup. Reduce the heat to low and continue to simmer, covered, for 3 hours. Add the parsley and farro during the last 30 minutes of cooking. Season to taste with salt and pepper and serve warm with the chermoula sauce.

Note: There are several ways to spike the soup with the Herby Chermoula. You can swirl it into the pot before serving to add an herby depth of flavor, or just add a dollop of sauce on top of each individual serving. If serving buffet style, place a bowl of chermoula next to the soup and let guests spoon the sauce into their soup bowls. That way, they can use as much as they like.

ROASTED CHICKEN NOODLE SOUP

Serves 8

Every time I roast a chicken I save the carcass to make this soup. If I can't make it right away, I freeze the carcass until I can. There is usually enough meat left on a carcass to add to the soup, so it's a budget-minded way to stretch two meals out of one chicken, and a perfect addition to this menu.

3 tablespoons olive oil
2 cups carrots (peeled and cut into coins)
1 cup chopped celery
1 small yellow onion, chopped
1 garlic clove, minced
1 cup chopped fresh Italian parsley
1 teaspoon salt
1 teaspoon pepper
6 cups chicken stock
1 (3- to 4-pound) roasted chicken (see recipe,
   page 152; you can use a carcass or whole roasted
   chicken)
2 cups dried egg noodles

In a large stockpot, heat the oil over medium heat. Add the carrots, celery, onion, and garlic and sauté for 3 minutes, or until the onion is translucent. Stir in the parsley and add the salt and pepper. Add the stock and 2 cups water and place the entire chicken in the pot. Bring to a simmer, then reduce the heat to low, and continue to simmer for 3 hours.

Once the broth is a golden color, remove the pot from the heat and use a slotted spoon to remove the chicken carcass from the soup. Using a fork and tongs, pull the meat off the bones (being careful not to burn yourself), and place the meat back into the soup pot. Add more stock if needed, and bring to a simmer over medium-low heat. Add the egg noodles and simmer for an additional 10 minutes. Serve hot.

GRILLED CHEESE SANDWICHES

with Brie, Crispy Bacon, and Apricot Jam

Serves 8

This is the best grilled cheese sandwich ever. Make them special by wrapping the quarters in parchment and lining them upright on a tray so guests can serve themselves.

2 loaves challah bread
8 pieces bacon, cooked crisp and crumbled
1 (12-ounce) wheel Brie cheese
8 tablespoons apricot jam
8 tablespoons butter, softened

Cut the challah into 16 slices.

To assemble the sandwiches, place 8 slices of the bread on a work surface. Top each slice with some of the crumbled bacon, a thin slice of Brie, and 1 tablespoon apricot jam. Cover each with 1 of the remaining 8 slices of bread, to make 8 sandwiches. Spread 1 tablespoon of the softened butter over the top slice of each sandwich.

In a medium or large sauté pan over medium heat, place 1 or 2 sandwiches, butter-side down, then butter the top slice. Cook until the bread is golden brown, then turn and cook the other side. Continue until all the sandwiches are cooked.

Allow the sandwiches to rest for 1 minute, then cut the sandwiches into quarters. Serve at room temperature.

Wrap individual quarters of grilled cheese sandwiches in parchment paper and tie them with butcher's string. Plate them on a narrow dish that contains the quarters in a row.

WHITE BEAN CHILI

Serves 8

This can be made a couple of days ahead and refrigerated in an airtight container until you are ready to heat and serve.

1 pound ground sirloin
1 pound ground turkey
3 tablespoons olive oil
1 small onion, chopped
3 garlic cloves, chopped
1/4 cup chili powder
1 teaspoon salt
1 teaspoon ground white pepper
1 teaspoon ground cinnamon
8 cups chicken stock
2 cups canned cannellini beans (drained and rinsed)
2 cups canned pinto beans (drained and rinsed)
2 tablespoons dried coriander

GARNISH
2 cups shredded white cheddar cheese
2 cups sour cream
4 avocados, peeled, pitted, and sliced
1 cup chopped fresh cilantro
1 (16-ounce) bag tortilla chips

In a stockpot over medium-high heat, sauté the ground sirloin and turkey for 5 minutes, or until browned. Use a slotted spoon to transfer the browned meat to a bowl and set aside. Pour any excess oil out of the pot.

Heat the olive oil in the same stockpot over medium heat. Add the onion and garlic and sauté for 3 to 5 minutes, until the onion is translucent. Add the browned meat back to the pot along with the chili powder, salt, pepper, and cinnamon. Pour in the stock and simmer for 1 hour. Add the cannellini and pinto beans and coriander and continue to simmer for 3 hours.

Serve with bowls of shredded cheese, sour cream, sliced avocado, chopped fresh cilantro, and tortilla chips alongside.

SAUSAGE AND PEPPERS

for a Crowd

Serves 8

This is a colorful dish to add to the table. Choose any kind of sausage you prefer, and if you need extra heat, just add more jalapeños. You can assemble this in the morning and refrigerate it, covered, until you are ready to cook. Just pop it in the oven an hour before guests arrive.

2 pounds (about 6 links) Italian sausages, sliced in bite-size rounds
2 red bell peppers, seeded, ribs removed, thinly sliced
2 green bell peppers, seeded, ribs removed, thinly sliced
1 (16-ounce) can crushed tomatoes
1/4 cup olive oil
2 hot banana peppers, sliced
1 fresh jalapeño, seeded and minced
4 garlic cloves, minced
1 teaspoon salt
Fresh rosemary, parsley, oregano, or chives, for garnish

Preheat the oven to 350° F.

Toss all the ingredients in a large bowl until well combined. Pour into a 15 x 10-inch ceramic baking dish and bake for 1 1/2 hours.

Garnish with your choice of fresh herbs.

A WORD ABOUT POTLUCK

I know many of you have grown up with the notion that bringing fully cooked dishes to friends' homes is perfectly normal. It's called "potluck," but I call it "NOT luck." This might seem harsh, but it is my feeling that asking friends to bring fully cooked side dishes to your home when you are the host is just not right.

None of these parties call for guests to bring anything to eat. It's difficult to know and coordinate what people will bring, and if the dish needs warming or further cooking, you may not have room on your cooktop.

As far as I'm concerned, the only time it is appropriate to bring fully cooked dishes to a friend's home is if they are sick and unable to cook, or if there's a new baby or a death in the family. To me, being a good host means that you do all the work and friends are welcome to bring a lovely hostess gift or bottles of good wine.

Sweets

PB & J THUMBPRINT COOKIES

Makes 24 to 32 cookies

Your guests will swoon over these if they are peanut butter-and-jelly fans. You can use your favorite jam, as long as it's red—color is important. The jam complements the color of the cookie and gives it more eye appeal.

1 cup whole wheat flour

1 teaspoon baking powder

3/4 teaspoon salt

1 cup smooth peanut butter

4 tablespoons unsalted butter, softened

1/2 cup sugar

1 large egg

1/2 cup chopped peanuts

1/2 cup strawberry jam, or your favorite red jam

Preheat the oven to 375° F.

Line 2 baking sheets with a Silpat or parchment paper. Sift the flour, baking powder, and salt together and set aside. In the bowl of a standing mixer fitted with the paddle attachment, beat together the peanut butter and butter on low speed to cream. Add the sugar and egg and beat until blended.

With the mixer running on low speed, slowly add the flour mixture and blend until all the ingredients are well incorporated. Add the chopped peanuts and beat on low speed for 10 seconds.

Transfer the dough to a work surface and roll into 1- to 2-inch balls with your hands.

Place the dough balls 2 inches apart on the prepared baking sheets, and use your thumb to press an indentation into the top of each dough ball.

Fill each indentation with 1 teaspoon strawberry jam, and bake the cookies for 12 minutes, or until golden brown. Transfer the cookies to a wire cooling rack to cool.

These cookies may be made in advance and stored at room temperature in a zip-top plastic bag for 3 days.

DEVIL'S FOOD CUPCAKES

Makes 2 dozen

You'll use 2 cupcake liners for each cupcake as part of the presentation of this dessert. The cupcakes are baked in traditional cupcake liners, then dropped into chocolate-brown paper baking cups for serving. For a pretty, monochromatic look, arrange the cupcakes on a wood tray lined with brown parchment paper.

1 cup good-quality cocoa powder

1 1/2 cups (3 sticks) unsalted butter, softened

2 cups sugar

4 large eggs

1 cup sour cream

1/4 cup canola oil

1 tablespoon vanilla extract

3 cups all-purpose flour

1 teaspoon baking soda

1 teaspoon salt

1 cup semisweet chocolate chips

CHOCOLATE FROSTING

3 cups sugar

7 tablespoons good-quality cocoa powder

1/2 cup (1 stick) unsalted butter, softened

6 tablespoons evaporated milk

For the cupcakes: Preheat the oven to 350° F.

Line 2 (12-cup) muffin tins with cupcake liners.

Heat a bowl with 1/2 cup water in the microwave on high for 30 seconds, then stir the cocoa powder into the hot water. Set the cocoa mixture aside.

In the bowl of a standing mixer fitted with a paddle attachment, combine the butter and sugar and beat for 2 minutes to cream. With the mixer on medium speed, add the eggs one at a time until incorporated. Then add the sour cream, oil, and vanilla. Add the cocoa mixture, and continue to blend on medium speed until combined.

In a separate mixing bowl, stir together the flour, baking soda, and salt. Add the dry mixture to the chocolate in the mixer and blend on low speed until incorporated. Next, add the chocolate chips on low speed to incorporate.

Fill each muffin cup three-quarters full with the batter and bake for 10 to 15 minutes, or until a toothpick inserted into the middle of a cupcake comes out clean. Allow the cupcakes to cool in the pan at room temperature for 2 hours before you frost them.

For the frosting: Sift the sugar and cocoa powder into a medium mixing bowl and set aside. In the bowl of a standing mixer fitted with a paddle attachment, beat the butter on medium speed to cream. With the mixer on low, add the sugar-cocoa mixture to the butter 1 cup at a time, alternating with 2 tablespoons of the evaporated milk, until all the cocoa mixture and milk are incorporated and the frosting is fluffy.

When the cupcakes have cooled, frost them using a small offset metal spatula, using 4 to 5 tablespoons of frosting per cupcake.

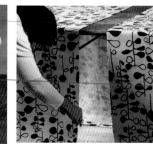

How to make a
DRAPERY TABLE RUNNER

MATERIALS:

96 x 36-inch patterned drapery panel
Pinking shears

DIRECTIONS:

1. Place the fabric panel down the length of your table.

2. Fold the panel in half lengthwise.

3. Cut down the fold using pinking shears.

4. Place both runners across the table so that they do not overlap.

How to make
HANDMADE NAPKINS

MATERIALS:

2 yards modern fabric to go with your
    color theme
Pinking shears

DIRECTIONS:

1. Cut one 16 x 16-inch square, then use the square as a template to cut out 7 more napkins with the same dimensions.

2. Fold each napkin and place in a small wooden crate on your buffet table.

Styling Secrets

PLACE PEANUT BUTTER-AND-JELLY COOKIES IN GIFT BAGS AND KEEP THEM NEAR YOUR FRONT DOOR AS A TAKE-HOME GIFT FOR GUESTS.

STACK MULTIPLE LOAVES OF BREAD ON A BREADBOARD AND PUT A LONG KNIFE THROUGH THEM TO CREATE A SCULPTURAL ELEMENT ON THE BUFFET TABLE.

USE BEAKERS TO HOLD BRANCHES FROM YOUR YARD AS A DRAMATIC CENTERPIECE.

STYLE A SEPARATE, SMALLER BUFFET WITH STOCKPOTS FULL OF HOT SOUP AND STACKED SOUP BOWLS AND SPOONS FOR EASY SELF-SERVICE. OR LEAVE THE STOCKPOTS ON THE STOVETOP WITH THE

STACKED SOUP BOWLS AND SPOONS NEARBY.

ELEMENTS

SERVING PIECES
3 sets of soup bowls, 8 in each set
8 small appetizer plates
Casserole, for sausage and peppers

GLASS
8 drinking glasses
5 glass beakers, for flowers: 2 small, 2 medium,
and 1 large (these are available online from a
scientific laboratory vendor)

METAL
Forks and spoons
3 pots for cooking and serving soup
3 ladles

TEXTILES
1 drapery panel, for table runner DIY project
2 yards modern fabric, for napkin DIY project

CERAMIC
1 narrow rectangular bowl, for grilled
cheese sandwiches
Vase for flowers
Bowl for chermoula sauce

WOOD
Cutting board for breads
Wood platter
Small wood crate, to hold napkins
Wood tray for cupcakes

PAPER + STRING
Parchment paper, to wrap grilled cheese
sandwiches
Butcher's string, to tie sandwiches
Small bags and tags, for takeaway gift cookies
Dark brown paper baking cups, for cupcakes
Brown parchment paper, to line tray for cupcakes

FLOWERS
Wildflowers and branches

THE WHITE PARTY

One of the first themed parties I ever attended was a "white party" in New York City. When we were first married my husband, Frank, and I lived in Manhattan. I found work as a window dresser, and was quickly surrounded by an amazing array of creative people. I was thrilled to be invited to my boss's home that winter for a party—and a white party to boot! We took great pains to figure out our outfits—this was a real New York–style event, with all the movers and shakers on the scene at that time, so we felt a little pressure. My friend Charlotte wore her wedding gown—she had been jilted at the altar, so what the heck—it was white and she had a sense of humor about it. A bawdy transplant from New Orleans, she was the life of the party that night.

My boss Al's Chelsea apartment was transformed. Every piece of furniture had been wrapped in white; white flowers covered the buffet and the bar. All the food and drinks were white. The effect was truly ethereal and magical.

When I moved to Atlanta, I recreated this fabulous party for our new friends in our new home. It was twenty-five years ago and to this day people still talk about that party. One of my husband's friends, an emergency room doctor, parked a vintage white ambulance in our front yard.

When you throw your own white party, remember to ask everyone to wear white. It adds to the décor and the mood. This party would be a great wedding shower or reception party, too. Your bright white party will make guests feel like they're in heaven.

The menu for this party includes store-bought items like cheese, honey, and sushi. Rounding up white food from the store makes perfect sense in this menu since the décor will take up more of your prep time.

menu

Champagne Cocktail

Goat Cheese Salad with Endive and Cucumber

Cheese and Honey Platter

Apple Cheddar Soufflés

White Shrimp and Grits with Crispy Sage

Assortment of sushi (store-bought)

Coconut Cake with Coconut Cream Cheese Frosting

CHAMPAGNE COCKTAIL

Makes 12

If you like a sweeter cocktail, add a sugar cube to each glass along with the bitters.

12 tablespoons elderflower liqueur (St. Germain)
12 lemon twists
12 champagne flutes
Bitters
2 bottles champagne or prosecco, chilled

Add 1 tablespoon of the liqueur and 1 lemon twist to each of 12 champage flutes. Add one drop of bitters to each glass. As guests arrive, fill each glass with champagne or prosecco and enjoy.

GOAT CHEESE SALAD
with Endive and Cucumber

Serves 10

CREAMY ITALIAN DRESSING

1 cup plain Greek-style yogurt

2 garlic cloves, minced

1/4 cup olive oil

1/2 teaspoon salt

Juice of 1 lemon

1 tablespoon dried parsley

1 tablespoon dried oregano

1 teaspoon dried basil

SALAD

3 cucumbers, peeled and sliced into 1/4-inch-thick
   rounds

5 bunches endive, cut crosswise into 1/4-inch-thick
   rounds

3 scallions, thinly sliced

1 small log soft fresh goat cheese, cut crosswise
   into 1/4-inch-thick rounds

For the dressing: Combine all the ingredients in a
jar with a lid and shake well until combined. The can
be made 1 day ahead and kept in the refrigerator.

   For the salad: In a large mixing bowl, toss the cucumbers, endive, and scallions to mix. Transfer to a
serving platter and garnish with the goat cheese
rounds. Pour half of the dressing over the salad,
and place the remainder of the dressing in a bowl
beside the salad for guests to serve themselves.

APPLE CHEDDAR SOUFFLÉS

Makes 24

*These bite-size soufflés are baked and served in
espresso cups. Be sure to let them cool a bit before your
guests handle them. Soufflés are often tricky to make,
so I recommend a test run before the party.*

   *The soufflés are unique because these can be made
ahead by filling espresso cups with batter, covering
them with plastic wrap, and freezing them for up to 3
days ahead of your party. Note: If you freeze them, do
not thaw them before baking; transfer the frozen soufflé cups directly to the preheated oven as directed.*

4 tablespoons unsalted butter, plus extra for
   greasing the espresso cups

1/4 cup all-purpose flour

1 1/4 cups whole milk

2 teaspoons chopped fresh rosemary

1/2 teaspoon salt

1/4 teaspoon pepper

10 ounces (1 1/2 cups) shredded sharp white
   cheddar cheese

1 Honeycrisp apple, peeled and grated

6 large eggs, separated

1/4 teaspoon cream of tartar

Preheat the oven to 375° F.

   Generously butter 24 oven-safe espresso cups
with butter, and place them 2 inches apart on 2
baking sheets.

   In a 2- to 3-quart pan over medium heat, melt
the butter. Add the flour and stir until the mixture
is smooth and bubbling. Stir in the milk, then add
the rosemary, salt, and pepper and continue stirring for 3 to 4 minutes, until the sauce comes to a
boil and thickens. Remove the pan from the heat,
add the cheddar cheese, and stir until it melts. Add
the grated apple and egg yolks, reserving the egg
whites in a separate bowl, and stir until the mixture
is smooth. Set aside.

   In a medium mixing bowl, using a standing mixer
fitted with a whisk attachment, beat the egg whites
with the cream of tartar on high speed until soft
peaks form. Using a flexible spatula, fold one third
of the cheese sauce into the egg whites and blend
well. Gently fold in the remaining sauce just until
blended.

   Fill the prepared espresso cups three-quarters
full with the batter and bake for 12 minutes, or until
the soufflé has risen and is golden brown. Serve
immediately.

Styling Secrets

ASK ALL YOUR GUESTS TO WEAR WHITE TO REINFORCE THE THEME.	POUR THE CHAM- PAGNE COCKTAILS AS SOON AS THE FIRST GUEST ARRIVES AND PLACE THEM ON THE BUFFET TABLE.	KEEP EVERYTHING ON THE TABLE AND ALL THE FOOD ITEMS WHITE—OR AS CLOSE AS POSSIBLE.	BAKE AND SERVE THE SOUFFLÉS IN ESPRESSO CUPS. YOU CAN BUY WHITE ESPRESSO CUPS AT A KITCHEN SUPPLY STORE FOR LESS THAN A DOLLAR APIECE.	SUSHI IS A GREAT PARTY FOOD AND A NATURAL FOR A WHITE PARTY. BUY READY- MADE CALIFORNIA ROLLS FROM A LOCAL SUSHI BAR OR GOUR- MET GROCER, AND	PLATE THEM ON A WHITE TRAY. SUSHI IS ALWAYS A CROWD- PLEASER AND ONE OF THOSE THINGS BEST PREPARED BY THE PROS ANYWAY.

A lot of the food items for this party can be purchased, like the sushi and the cheese-and-honey platter. Create a beautiful cheese platter by placing the cheese on a white plate atop a white marble slab. Arrange the crackers and nuts on either side. Place a honeycomb on a separate ceramic board or tile, along with a honey server. Texture is really important when building your cheese platter.

WHITE SHRIMP AND GRITS

with Crispy Sage

Serves 12

GRITS
8 cups whole milk

8 cups chicken stock

4 cups white stone-ground grits

2 cup grated Parmesan cheese

1/2 cup (1 stick) unsalted butter, melted

2 teaspoons salt

SHRIMP
6 tablespoons olive oil

4 pounds (60 count) medium shrimp, peeled
and deveined

4 garlic cloves, minced

2 cup chicken stock

1/2 cup dry white wine

2 teaspoons salt

1 teaspoon white pepper

CRISPY SAGE LEAVES
1 cup olive oil

2 cup fresh sage leaves

For the grits: In a large saucepan over high heat, bring the milk and stock to a boil and whisk in the grits. Reduce the heat to low and cook uncovered for 40 to 50 minutes, whisking often, until the grits are creamy. Whisk in the cheese, butter, and salt, then cover and set aside.

For the shrimp: Heat the olive oil in a large skillet over medium heat and cook the shrimp until they are pink. Using a slotted spoon, remove the shrimp from the pan and set aside.

Add the garlic to the oil left in the skillet, sauté for 1 minute, then add the stock, white wine, salt, and pepper and cook over medium heat until the broth is reduced to half its volume.

Remove from the heat, return the shrimp to the broth in the pan, and cover to keep warm.

For the sage leaves: Heat the oil in a small sauté pan over high heat and fry the sage leaves for 3 to

5 minutes, stirring, until they are golden brown. Remove with a slotted spoon and drain on paper towels. To serve, ladle the warm grits into individual bowls, top each bowl with some of the shrimp mixture, and crumble a few crispy sage leaves on each serving.

COCONUT CAKE

with Coconut Cream Cheese Frosting

Serves 10 to 12

This cake has the dense crumb of a pound cake. When you frost it, the cake looks very much like a giant snowball. You can make the cake ahead and store it in the freezer wrapped in plastic wrap. Thaw overnight and frost it the morning of the party. Place the frosted cake unwrapped in the refrigerator and remove from the refrigerator 3 hours before guests arrive.

CAKE
1 cup (2 sticks) unsalted butter, softened, plus extra
for greasing the cake pans

2 cups sugar

5 large eggs, at room temperature

1 teaspoon vanilla extract

1 teaspoon coconut extract

3 cups all-purpose flour, plus extra for flouring the
cake pans

1 teaspoon baking powder

1/2 teaspoon baking soda

1/2 teaspoon salt

1 1/2 cups whole milk

Juice of 1 lemon

5 ounces sweetened shredded moist coconut

FROSTING
1 (8-ounce) package cream cheese, softened

1 cup (2 sticks) unsalted butter, softened

1 teaspoon vanilla extract

1 teaspoon coconut extract

1/2 teaspoon salt

5 cups confectioners' sugar

ASSEMBLY
3/4 cup prepared lemon curd for the filling, your
favorite brand

16 ounces (2 cups) sweetened shredded moist coconut

For the cake: Preheat the oven to 350° F. Grease 2 (9-inch) cake pans with butter and dust with flour.

In the bowl of a standing mixer fitted with a paddle, cream the butter and sugar on low speed for 2 to 3 minutes, or until creamy. With the mixer still on low speed, add the eggs one at a time, then add the vanilla and coconut extract and blend until smooth.

In a separate mixing bowl, sift together the flour, baking powder, baking soda, and salt. Add the dry ingredients to the butter mixture in the bowl of the mixer on low speed, and blend for 2 minutes, or until well combined.

Stir together the milk and lemon juice in a cup, and add that to the mixer, then add the coconut.

Divide the batter between the prepared pans and bake for 45 minutes, or until a knife inserted into the middle of the cakes comes out clean. Allow the cakes to cool in the pans for 30 minutes, then turn them out onto a wire cooling rack to cool completely.

For the frosting: Mix the cream cheese and butter in the bowl of a standing mixer fitted with the paddle attachment on low speed. With the mixer running, add the vanilla, coconut extract, and salt, then slowly add the confectioners' sugar and mix until completely combined.

To assemble and frost the cake: Place 1 cake layer, flat-side down, on a cake plate. Use a bread (serrated) knife to slice a thin layer off the rounded top of the cake to flatten it. Spread the 3/4 cup lemon curd evenly across the top of the cake and allow the cake to stand for 5 minutes, or until the curd sets up. Then spread a 1/2-inch layer of frosting on top of the curd. Sprinkle with 1/4 cup sweetened coconut, then place the second layer, flat-side down, atop the first. Before the final frosting is applied, frost the entire cake with a crumb coat (a very thin layer of frosting applied to a cake before the final frosting is applied, essentially trapping all the loose crumbs on the surface of the cake in a thin layer of frosting) and refrigerate for 20 minutes.

Remove the cake from the refrigerator and apply the final frosting to cover the entire cake. Using your hands, press the remaining shredded coconut over the cake to evenly coat.

How to make a
FUR TABLECLOTH

MATERIALS:

About 3 yards (36- to 42-inch
wide) white fur fabric
(measure your table to
determine the length to buy)
Scissors

DIRECTIONS:

Spread the fur fabric out on
your buffet table and cut the fur
to fit the table. If the fur is wide
enough, allow extra fur as a
drop on the sides of the table.

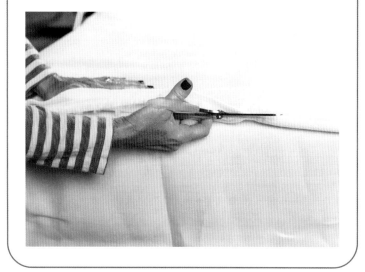

How to make
WHITE FLOWER ARRANGEMENTS

MATERIALS:

3 to 4 white ceramic vases, in
   varying heights
3 bunches of white peonies
   (I buy them with the buds
   closed 4 days before the
   party and place them in
   water. It takes about 4 days
   for them to open to full bloom.)
Scissors

DIRECTIONS:

1. Fill each vase halfway with
water.

2. Lay the flowers out on a
table and trim the stems so that
the blossoms reach just above
the lip of each vase.

3. Place at least 3 blooms in
each vase.

ELEMENTS

SERVING PIECES
12 plates
12 dessert plates
1 glass pitcher
12 champagne flutes

METAL
Tongs for sushi
Appetizer knives, for cheese platter
Salad servers
Cake server

TEXTILES
12 white napkins

CERAMIC
Bowl for shrimp and grits
24 espresso cups for soufflé
Long rectangular platters, for folded napkins
3 white vases

STONE
2 marble cake stands: 1 for cake, 1 for
elevating grits bowl
1 marble slab, for cheeses and honey

WOOD
Candlestick
Honey server

PLASTIC
White tray, for sushi
White bowl, for salad

PAPER + STRING
Paper garland (see Source Guide, page 222)
Paper pom-poms (see Source Guide, page 222)
Paper fans (see Source Guide, page 222)
Tags to label dishes

LIGHTING + ILLUMINATION
Candlesticks and candles

FLOWERS
3 bunches fresh white peonies

GAME DAY
pizza party

I have saved the best party for last. This is a party that never misses. Guests get to design and make their own pizzas—you just have all the ingredients and the dough ready for them. Every time I throw this party it's a huge hit because it's so much fun for everyone to get into the kitchen and make pizzas. If I haven't had one of these parties in a while, one of my best friends, Jerry, begs me to plan one. Jerry is always the first in line and makes the most insane pizza topping combinations, such as pineapple, anchovy, and blue cheese.

Rolling out your own pizza dough is fun and gets everyone involved. Everyone feels like a chef when food is this easy to prepare. You'd be surprised how many people who've never boiled water will have a real sense of accomplishment when they've made their own pizza.

Everyone slices their pizza and trades slices with other guests, and the conversation about whose pizza is best is as lively as the sports talk.

After guests have eaten, I like to clean up and lay out the dessert pizza selections. We start again with combinations and taste tests.

This party is great for a child's birthday party, too—it's been a big hit with my son and his friends.

menu

Big Game Snack Mix

Create-Your-Own Pizza

Nutella Banana Calzone

Fruit Dessert Pizza

SUPER PIZZA CRUST

Makes 6 to 8 (12-inch) pizza crusts

You will need to make 2 batches of this pizza—one for the savory and one for the dessert pizzas/calzones. Prepare all the dough in the morning so you have time to let it rise. Cover the dough and let it sit at room temperature until the guests arrive. An hour before guests arrive, cut the first batch of dough into 12 parts and roll out (3-inch diameter) balls, then place them back into the bowl for guests to help themselves.

1 cup warm water
2 packages active dry yeast
6 cups all-purpose flour (for a whole wheat option, use 4 cups all-purpose flour and 2 cups whole wheat flour)
1 cup olive oil, plus extra for oiling the bowl
2 1/2 teaspoons salt

In the bowl of a standing mixer fitted with a dough hook, mix the 1 cup warm water and the yeast on low speed for 30 seconds. Allow the yeast to proof, or sit, for 10 minutes. Add the flour, oil, and salt and blend on low speed for 2 minutes. Add more warm water if the dough is dry and won't hold together.

Note: You can also mix the dough by hand. Following the recipe directions, this technique will take about 5 minutes. The dough should be smooth and elastic to the touch.

Transfer the dough to a large oiled mixing bowl and knead it for 10 to 20 seconds, then form it into a ball. Cover the bowl tightly with plastic wrap, and let the dough rise for 1 hour on the kitchen counter.

When it has risen, punch the dough down with your fist, cover again with plastic wrap, and allow it to rise for another hour. At this point it can sit out safely at room temperature for 2 more hours.

Repeat this entire recipe to make the second batch of dough for the dessert pizzas.

BIG GAME SNACK MIX

Makes 10 (1 cup) servings

You can find wasabi peas and Asian snack mix at specialty food stores, Asian markets, and well-stocked gorcery stores.

2 cups wasabi peas
2 cups roasted almonds
3 cups garlic crackers
3 cups mixed Asian snack mix

Toss all the ingredients together in a large bowl and serve.

To Assemble:

1. Make the 2 batches of pizza dough according to the recipe.

2. Cut 24 individual pieces of parchment paper into 16 x 16-inch squares—you will need 2 squares per guest.

3. When the dough has risen a second time, use a knife to cut pieces from the risen dough and roll the dough into 3-inch individual balls. Stack them in a large wooden bowl on a workspace where guests can roll them out to make individual pizzas. Stack the parchment paper squares next to the pizza dough balls for easy access.

4. Set out all the savory toppings on a counter or on the kitchen table for easy access.

5. Preheat the oven to 500° F.

6. Place the toppings next to the bowl of dough balls and parchment paper squares.

7. Have an open work surface clean and ready for guests to flatten their dough on a square of parchment and assemble their custom pizzas, using toppings of their choice.

8. As guests finish assembling their pizzas, place them in the oven on their parchment squares. You will need to station yourself at the oven to monitor pizzas while they are cooking Note: You should be able to fit 2 pizzas into a standard oven.

9. Bake each pizza for 5 minutes, or until the crust begins to brown, then remove from the oven and let the pizza sit for 3 to 5 minutes to cool slightly. Guests can slice and eat their pizza on the parchment paper.

SUGGESTED TOPPINGS

Cheeses Parmesan, cheddar, packaged mozzarella, fresh mozzarella, goat cheese, feta, blue cheese crumbles

Sauces tomato and pesto

Salsas tomato or mango

Meats sausage, chorizo, prosciutto, salami, pepperoni, ham, cooked ground sausage

Vegetables grilled zucchini, grilled mushrooms, roasted red peppers, sliced red onions, asparagus, roasted garlic, fresh chopped garlic

Olives green and black, pitted and sliced

Oils truffle oil, hot pepper oil

Tapenades olive, sun-dried tomato

Greens arugula, spinach, radicchio

Sliced fresh tomatoes

Assorted herbs

Fruit Sliced pears

INSTRUCTIONS FOR GUESTS TO MAKE THEIR INDIVIDUAL PIZZAS

(You may want to print these out for guests to refer to as they make their pizzas.)

1. On a flat work surface, place 1 dough ball on a parchment square.

2. Form the pizza crust by pressing the dough ball out with your palms and fingers to form a 12-inch disk.

3. Select any topping combination that you desire, and layer or arrange them on top of the pizza dough. There are no rules to this part!

4. Place the pizza and the parchment paper directly on a rack in the oven and bake for 5 minutes, or until the cheese is bubbling and the edges of the dough are crispy.

5. Remove the pizza and parchment paper from the oven and allow it to rest for 3 to 5 minutes before slicing and eating.

Note: Have pizza cutters available for guests to slice their own pizzas. It cuts down on the kitchen work you need to do.

How to make a
POM-POM CENTERPIECE

Place these in the center of the table, or even on a coffee table decorated for the game. You can buy the paper pom-poms in a multitude of colors, which makes it easy to find your team's colors.

MATERIALS:

3 to 4 (6-inch diameter) paper pom-poms, available from Amazon.com or at a party store
3 to 4 striped paper straws
Hot-glue gun
3 to 4 vintage Thermos bottles, found at flea markets or available online

DIRECTIONS:

1. Heat the hot-glue gun. Put hot glue on the end of the straw and glue the straw in the center of the pom-pom.

2. Allow the glue to dry before placing the pom-poms in the vintage Thermoses.

Styling Secrets

PLACE ALL THE PIZZA TOPPINGS ON AS MANY OVAL-SHAPED BOWLS AND PLATTERS AS POSSIBLE, TO SUGGEST THE SHAPE OF A FOOTBALL.

STOCK THE SPACE IN YOUR REFRIGERATOR AS AN ORGANIZED SELF-SERVE BAR. CHILL BEER MUGS AND STOCK WITH ARTISAN BEER AND SOFT DRINKS THAT GUESTS CAN HELP THEMSELVES TO THROUGHOUT THE GAME.

USE MARKERS TO LABEL CRATES FOR ARUGULA, LETTUCE, AND HERB TOPPINGS. MARK THE TYPE OF GREENS ON THE PENDANTS WITH A SHARPIE.

Dessert pizzas: Once guests have enjoyed their entrée pizza, you can cut the second bowl of pizza dough into 12 (3-inch diameter) balls. Place these near the dessert toppings and the parchment paper squares for guests to assemble as before.

NUTELLA BANANA CALZONE

Makes 1

This is something I prefer to make for guests because it's a little more complicated, but if guests want to try it, by all means let them. You can serve one of these per person, or cut each one into three servings and pass them around on a plate.

1 (3-inch) dough ball from Pizza Crust recipe
   (page 208), for crust
3 tablespoons Nutella chocolate-hazelnut spread
1/2 banana, sliced into 1/4-inch-thick slices
Confectioners' sugar, for dusting

Preheat the oven to 500° F.

   Place a dough ball on a parchment square on a flat work surface.

   Form the pizza crust by pressing the dough ball out with your palms and fingers to form a 12-inch disk. Spread 3 tablespoons Nutella over half of the dough round, top with the banana slices, then fold the dough in half over the banana slices and crimp the edges together with your fingers.

   Bake for 5 minutes on the parchment paper, or until golden brown.

   Allow the Nutella pizza to sit at room temperature for 10 minutes to cool, then sprinkle with confectioners' sugar and serve.

FRUIT DESSERT PIZZA

These are easy pizzas for your guests to make themselves. Have the dessert pizza ingredients laid out in bowls for guests to choose. And by all means, add any ingredients you like to this list!

Suggested toppings

Fruit compotes, your favorite brands
1 jar Nutella chocolate-hazelnut spread
Cinnamon
Sugar
Honey
1 pineapple, sliced
Peaches, sliced
Strawberries, sliced
Apricots, sliced
Plain Greek-style yogurt, for topping
Granola
Nuts

Preheat the oven to 500° F.

   Place a dough ball on a parchment square on a flat work surface.

   Form the pizza crust by pressing the dough ball out with your palms and fingers to form a 12-inch disk.

   Place the disk and the parchment paper in the oven and brown, about 5 minutes.

   Let the pizza crust cool for 5 minutes, then top with plain Greek yogurt, fresh fruit and honey, nuts, or whatever you desire.

Clockwise from upper left: Grilled Veggie Pizza: grilled zucchini, grilled squash, grilled red peppers, grilled asparagus, fresh mushrooms, crumbled fresh goat cheese; Pear and Blue Cheese Pizza: sliced fresh pears, blue cheese crumbles, fresh arugula, sliced red onion, and thinly sliced radicchio garnish; Classic Margarita Pizza: olive oil, minced garlic, sliced tomatoes, fresh mozzarella slices, salt and pepper to taste, and fresh basil leaf garnish; Mexi-Pizza: salsa, black beans, sliced jalapeños, cooked crumbled sausage or chorizo, shredded cheddar cheese, crumbled queso fresco, and fresh cilantro garnish.

How to make
PENNANT CRATES

MATERIALS:

3 (4- x 4-inch) cardboard produce crates,
   available from a farmers' market, or ask
   your grocer if they save them to recycle
Colorful duct tape
Scissors

DIRECTIONS:

1. Cut a 4-inch length of duct tape.

2. Stick the top 1/2-inch of the tape to the
top lip of the crate, leaving a 4-inch flag
of tape.

3. Evenly fold half the length of the tape
under and press the tape together tightly
to form a 2-inch square tape flag that is
stuck on the lip of the crate.

4. Cut the square tape into a triangle by
finding the center point of the square and
cutting out toward the crate at a diagonal
on either side to form a triangle.

5. You can write on this tab with a Sharpie
if you wish to label the toppings in each
container.

How to make a
PENNANT GARLAND

MATERIALS:

8 to 10 feet of butcher's string
2 rolls colorful duct tape in your team
   colors
Scissors

DIRECTIONS:

1. Cut the string to a length that is long
enough to hang over your table.

2. Place the string on a work surface and
cut the colorful duct tape into 4-inch
lengths.

3. Evenly fold half the length of the tape
over the string and press the tape together tightly to form a square. Repeat,
placing the pennant tape equal distances
apart on the string.

4. Cut each tape square into a triangle to
form the shape of a pennant, starting at
the middle of the square and cutting diagonally toward the string on both sides.

ELEMENTS

SERVING PIECES
3 to 4 pizza cutters

GLASS
12 beer mugs, chilled

METAL
Tray, for fruit for dessert pizza
3 to 4 vintage Thermoses, for pom-pom
centerpieces

TEXTILES
Napkins

CERAMIC
Large bowl, for snack mix
6 bowls, for sauces, salsas, tapenades, and olives

WOOD
6 medium bowls, for pizza toppings
3 wooden plates, for meat and cheese
pizza toppings
5 wooden utensils, for serving toppings
4 wooden forks, for serving toppings

PAPER + RIBBON + STRING
3 small cardboard produce crates, for herbs
and lettuce
Parchment paper, for rolling out and baking pizza
dough, pre-cut into 24 (16-inch) squares
Butcher's string
2 rolls colorful duct tape in team colors,
for labeling produce crates and
making pennant garland
3 to 4 paper pom-poms
3 to 4 paper stripe straws

How to make a
FOOTBALL FIELD TABLE RUNNER

MATERIALS:

1 (2-foot-width) piece of ¼-inch-thick natural
   veneer, the length of the table you intend to
   use
1 (12-ounce) can of green chalkboard
   spray paint, available at the hardware store
1 container of sidewalk chalk, available at the
   craft store
1 small disposable paint roller
Small pan
Soft cloth
Straight-edge ruler

DIRECTIONS:

1. Using a roller, paint one side of the board
and allow it to dry. It may need 2 coats of
paint.

2. Once the paint dries, prime the board
using a piece of white chalk, and covering the
board in broad chalk strokes.

3. Using a soft cloth, rub off most of the
chalk to create a soft, chalky look.

4. With a straight-edged ruler and a piece of
white sidewalk chalk, draw evenly spaced
lines the width of the board to create the look
of a football field.

5. Place in the center of the buffet table.

Index

a

acorn squash soup, 162
affogato, 84
aioli, red pepper, 177
ambiance, 134. *See also* décor
The Americano, 126
apple
    cheddar soufflés, 198
    pear and dried fig whole wheat
        cobbler, 145
    pie, 111, 120
arrabbiata sauce, 94
arugula salad
    beet and goat cheese, 142
    blueberry and, 70
    with parmesan shavings, 82
asparagus, grilled, 32

b

baby showers, 41
bacon
    grilled brie sandwiches with apricot
        jam and crispy, 187
    pear and walnut stuffing, 164
bags
    bread and olive, 146
    cactus, 61
barbecue ribs, Dr. Frank's favorite, 118
basil
    caprese salad, 94, 174, 175
    corn and tomato salad with fresh, 114
    cream, 174
    pesto oil, 130
beans, black, slow-cooked, 61. *See also*
        white bean
beef brisket soft tacos, Coca-Cola ancho
        chile pulled, 60
beet and goat cheese salad, 142
berries. *See* blueberry; raspberry;
        strawberry

biscotti, rosemary, 84
blueberry
    and arugula salad, 70
    pie, 74
    trifle, 48
bread
    bags, 146
    crostini, 30
    croutons, 57, 162
    pita, 104, 177
    pizza crust, super, 208–209
    sun-dried tomato and olive, 151
bread pudding, pumpkin, 166, 167
breadsticks, prosciutto-wrapped, 126
brie sandwiches, grilled, with crispy
        bacon and apricot jam, 187
broccoli rabe, hot garlic, 152
bruschetta, grilled vegetable, 43
burgers, mini tzatziki lamb, 104

c

cake
    coconut, 200
    devil's food, 190
    limoncello cheesecake parfaits, 106
calamari salad in pesto oil, 130
Campari, 123, 126, 132
candy cane martini, 174
cannoli, deconstructed raspberry, 36
caprese salad, 94, 174, 175
centerpieces, 27, 30, 144, 156, 168, 210
champagne cocktail, 197
charcuterie platter, 140
cheese
    apple cheddar soufflés, 198
    caprese salad, 94, 174, 175
    charcuterie platter with, 140
    goat, and beet salad, 142
    goat, grilled vegetable bruschetta
        with, 43
    goat, salad with endive and
        cucumber, 198

grilled brie sandwiches with crispy
        bacon and apricot jam, 187
parmesan crisps, 94
as pizza topping, 210
platters, 199
ricotta-stuffed fried squash blossoms,
        77, 80–81
cheesecake parfaits, limoncello, 106
chermoula sauce, 186
chicken
    noodle soup, roasted, 186
    roast, 152
children, 41, 163, 171, 205
chili, white bean, 188
chocolate chip cookies, 154
chocolate frosting, 190
Christmas. *See* holiday cocktail open
        house
Cinco de Mayo parties
    about, 55
    elements of, 55, 58, 61, 62, 64–65
    menu for, 57–62
cinnamon ice cream sundae, 62
cobbler, apple, pear, and dried fig whole
        wheat, 145
Coca-Cola ancho chile pulled brisket soft
        tacos, 60
cocktails. *See* drinks; holiday cocktail
        open house
coconut
    cake, 200
    cream cheese frosting, 200
    sour cream, 58
comfort food get-togethers
    about, 183
    elements of, 192–193
    menu for, 185–190
cookies
    chocolate chip, 154
    PB & J thumbprint, 190
    pignoli, 132
corn and tomato salad, 114

cranberry sauce, kumquat, 166
cream cheese frosting, coconut, 200
crêpes with Nutella, mini, 178
crostini, 30
croutons, 57, 162
cucumber
    goat cheese salad with endive and, 198
    slaw, 104
cupcakes, devil's food, 190

d

décor. *See also* elements; lighting; linens
    bags, 61, 146
    centerpieces, 27, 30, 144, 156, 168, 210
    flower, 68, 96, 134, 156, 202
    garlands, 181, 214
    as guest activity, 41
    holiday, 180-181
    painting, 41, 50-52
    pennants, 214
    place cards, 163
dessert. *See also* cookies; ice cream; pie
    bread pudding, pumpkin, 166, 167
    cake, coconut, 200
    calzone, Nutella banana, 213
    cannoli, deconstructed raspberry, 36
    cobbler, apple, pear, and dried fig whole wheat, 145
    cookies, pignoli, 132
    crêpes with Nutella, mini, 178
    cupcakes, devil's food, 190
    devil's food cupcakes, 190
    nests, 48
    parfaits, limoncello cheesecake, 106
    pavlova, mini, 178-179
    pizza, fruit, 213
    sorbet, Campari-orange, 132
    tiramisu, strawberry, 98
    trifle, 48
dinner parties. *See* comfort food get-togethers; Sunday supper;

Thanksgiving celebration
dressing. *See* salad dressing
drinks
    The Americano, 126
    candy cane martini, 174
    champagne cocktail, 197
    dry martini, 126
    the ginger snap cocktail, 162
    lime-y thyme-y gin, 126
    limoncello sangria, 174
    spa water, 106

e

Easter lunch
    about, 41
    elements, 41, 46, 48, 50-53
    menu, 41-48
elements, 13-23
    Cinco de Mayo party, 55, 58, 61, 62, 64-65
    comfort food get-together, 192-193
    Easter lunch, 41, 46, 48, 50-53
    essential list of, 13, 15
    Fourth of July picnic, 111, 114, 116, 118, 120
    game day pizza party, 210, 214-215
    holiday cocktail open house, 171, 174, 175, 180-181
    Italian spring feast, 82, 87
    Memorial Day cookout, 67, 68, 70, 72, 75
    organizing, 13-23
    Palio celebration, 92, 94, 95, 96, 98
    preparation of, 14, 16
    repurposing, 11, 13
    retro Riviera party, 128, 132, 134-135
    spring garden party, 27, 30, 32, 34, 36, 39
    summer pool grill-out, 104, 105, 107, 108
    Sunday supper, 149, 152, 154, 156
    Thanksgiving celebration, 159, 163, 164, 168-169
    white party, 195, 198, 202-203

wine harvest party, 140, 142, 144, 146
entertaining. *See* parties

f

fall. *See* Sunday supper; Thanksgiving celebration; wine harvest parties
farro
    salad with olives and pink grapefruit, 45
    soup, white bean vegetable, 186
fig, apple, pear whole wheat cobbler, 145
fish. *See also* seafood
    grilled whole rainbow trout, 34
    grilled whole salmon, 96
flowers
    arrangement of, 68, 96, 202
    vases for, 134, 156
food styling, 8, 16. *See also* elements
Fourth of July picnic
    about, 111
    elements, 111, 114, 116, 118, 120
    menu, 112-120
fries, sweet potato oven, 106
frittatas, mini, 130
frosting
    chocolate, 190
    coconut cream cheese, 200
fruit. *See also* specific fruits
    dessert pizza, 213
    grilled, 58, 114
    trifle, individual, 48
frutti di mare, pasta, 128

g

galette, potato, 44
game day pizza parties. *See also* Palio celebration
    about, 205
    elements of, 210, 214-215
    menu for, 207-213
garden parties. *See* spring garden parties
garlands, 181, 214
gazpacho, chilled, 57

gift food, takeaway, 120, 151, 166, 171, 178, 180, 192
gin, lime-y thyme-y, 126
the ginger snap cocktail, 162
goat cheese. See cheese
graduation parties, 41
grapefruit, pink, farro salad with olives and, 45
gravy, roasted vegetable, 164
Greek salad, big fat, 104
green beans, 166
grilled asparagus, 32
grilled brie sandwiches, 187
grilled flank steak, 72
grilled mini tzatziki lamb burgers, 104
grilled pea soup shooters, 69
grilled peaches, 114
grilled pineapple, 58
grilled vegetable bruschetta, 43
grilled whole rainbow trout, 34
grilled whole salmon, 96
grits, white shrimp and, 200
guacamole, 58
guests
    activities for, 41, 68, 205, 210
    clothing and accessories for, 89, 132, 197
    greeting, 126, 162
    place cards for, 163
    self-serve by, 60, 104, 167, 187, 210
    takeaway gift food for, 120, 151, 166, 171, 178, 180, 192

h

holiday cocktail open house
    about, 171
    elements, 171, 174, 175, 180-181
    menu, 173-179
holidays. See Cinco de Mayo parties; Easter lunch; Fourth of July picnic; Memorial Day cookout
horse races, 89

i

ice cream
    Campari-orange sorbet, 132
    lavender, 74
    olive oil–vanilla affogato, 84
    sandwiches, homemade chocolate chip, 154
    sundae, homemade cinnamon, 62
Independence Day. See Fourth of July picnic
Italian chopped salad, 128
Italian salad dressing, creamy, 70, 198
Italian spring feast
    about, 77
    elements, 82, 87
    menu, 78-84
Italy, 45, 77, 84, 88, 98, 123, 130, 145

j

jam
    grilled brie sandwiches with crispy bacon and apricot, 187
    PB & J thumbprint cookies, 190
    sweet pepper, 140
    tomato, 94
Joseph, Annette, 8, 27, 41, 77, 101, 111, 123, 137, 159
Joseph, Frank, 118, 159, 195

k

kale, Tuscan sweet and sour, 44
Kentucky Derby parties, 89
kumquat cranberry sauce, 166

l

lamb
    burgers, mini tzatziki, 104
    roast leg of, 46
lavender ice cream, 74
leftovers, 164, 186
lemon(s)

grilled whole salmon with tomatoes, zucchini and, 96
herb stuffing, 46
leaf floral wreath, 96
risotto shrimp "cocktails," 176–177
shallot vinaigrette, 32
lighting
    candle pots, 152
    lanterns, 114
    silver luminaries, 61
    string, 116
    votives, 82, 168
lime
    thyme-lime dressing, 142
    thyme-y gin, 126
limoncello
    cheesecake parfaits, 106
    sangria, 174
linens
    dying, 55, 64
    napkins, 36, 50, 64, 72, 114, 140, 168, 192
    painting, 51-52
    scarves, 89
    soda wraps, 70
    table runners, 94, 108, 118, 144, 192, 215
    tablecloths, 27, 41, 52, 64, 82, 202
lunches. See Easter lunch; Fourth of July picnic; spring garden parties

m

mandarin oil, 32, 34
marinades
    Dr. Frank's favorite barbecue ribs, 118
    grilled whole salmon, 96
    roast leg of lamb, 46
    sun-dried tomato steak, 72
martinis
    candy cane, 174
    dry, 126
Memorial Day cookout
    about, 67

elements, 67, 68, 70, 72, 75
menu, 68-74
menus
    Cinco de Mayo party, 57-62
    comfort food get-together, 185-190
    Easter lunch, 41-48
    Fourth of July picnic, 112-120
    game day pizza party, 207-213
    holiday cocktail open house, 173-179
    Italian spring feast, 78-84
    Memorial Day cookout, 68-74
    Palio celebration, 90-98
    retro Riviera party, 125-132
    spring garden party, 29-36
    summer pool grill-out, 103-106
    Sunday supper, 149, 150-154
    Thanksgiving, 161-166
    white party, 195, 197-200
    wine harvest party, 139-142, 145
    writing and posting, 149, 156
meringue, mini pavlova, 178-179
Mexican food. See Cinco de Mayo parties
mushrooms
    green beans with crispy shallots and, 166
    porcini risotto, 151
music, 134
mussels
    pasta frutti di mare, 128
    in white wine, 92

n

napkins, 36, 50, 64, 72, 114, 140, 168, 192
Nutella
    banana calzone, 213
    mini crêpes with, 178

o

office parties, 171
oil
    lemon, 82
    mandarin, 32, 34

olive, vanilla ice cream, 32, 34
    pesto, 130
    pizza topping, 210
    truffle, 82, 178
olive(s)
    bags, 146
    bread, sun-dried tomato and, 151
    farro salad with pink grapefruit and, 45
    pizza topping, 210
    tapenade, 30, 210
    warm marinated, 126
onions
    crispy, 61
    pickled, 72, 140
open house. See holiday cocktail open house

p

painting, 41, 50-52
Palio celebration
    about, 89
    elements, 92, 94, 95, 96, 98
    menu, 90-98
pantry supplies, 13-23. See also elements
parfaits, limoncello cheesecake, 106
parmesan crisps, 94
parties
    baby shower, 41
    children and, 41, 163, 171, 205
    Cinco de Mayo, 55-65
    comfort food get-togethers, 183-193
    cost of, 10, 11
    easiest, 137, 182
    Easter lunch, 41-53
    Fourth of July picnic, 111-120
    game day pizza, 205-215
    graduation, 41
    holiday cocktail open house, 171-181
    Italian spring feast, 77-87
    Joseph's, Annette, background on, 8
    Kentucky Derby, 89
    Memorial Day cookout, 67-75

office, 171
Palio celebration, 89-98
pantry supplies for, 13-23
potluck, 188
preparation for, 14, 16
retro Riviera, 123-135
spa, 101
spring garden, 27-39
summer pool grill-out, 101-108
Sunday supper, 149-156
Thanksgiving, 159-169
white, 195-203
wine harvest, 137-146
pasta
    frutti di mare, 128
    penne, with arrabbiata sauce, 94
    roasted chicken noodle soup, 186
    spaghettini with zucchini coins, speck and truffle oil, 82
    white bean and kale soup with, 142
pavlovas, mini, 178-179
PB & J thumbprint cookies, 190
pea soup shooters, grilled, 69
peaches, grilled, 114
pear
    apple and dried fig whole wheat cobbler, 145
    pizza topping, 210
    walnut and bacon stuffing, 164
pennants, 214
penne pasta with arrabbiata sauce, 94
pepper. See red pepper
pesto oil, 130
photography, 8
pickled onions, 72, 140
pickles, sweet, 140
picnics. See Fourth of July picnic
pie
    apple, 111, 120
    blueberry, 74
pignoli cookies, 132
pineapple, grilled, 58

pipettes, 174, 175
pita bread, 104, 177
pizza
    crust, super, 208–209
    dessert, fruit, 213
    guests creating own, 205, 210
    Nutella banana calzone, 213
    toppings, 210
place cards, 163
polenta, oven-baked, 70
pool parties. See summer pool grill-out
popcorn, 178, 180
porcini mushroom risotto, 151
pork ribs, Dr. Frank's favorite barbecue, 118
potato
    galette, 44
    salad, red, white and blue, 116
    sweet, oven fries, 106
potlucks, 188
prosciutto-wrapped breadsticks, 126
pumpkin bread pudding, 166, 167

r

radishes, blueberry and arugula salad
    with sweet, 70
raspberry
    cannoli, deconstructed, 36
    trifle, 48
red pepper
    aioli, 177
    coulis, tomato-, 130
    jam, sweet, 140
    sausage and, 188
    the stand up salad, 176
repurposing, 11, 13
retro Riviera parties
    about, 123
    elements of, 128, 132, 134–135
    menu for, 125–132
ribs, Dr. Frank's favorite barbecue, 118
ricotta-stuffed fried squash blossoms, 77,
    80–81

risotto
    lemony, 176–177
    porcini mushroom, 151
roast beef with red pepper aioli in pita
    bread, 177
roast chicken, 152
roast leg of lamb, 46
roast turkey, 164
roasted shrimp and tomatoes, herb-, 131
roasted vegetable gravy, 164
rosemary biscotti, 84

s

sage
    crispy, 200
    croutons, 162
salad
    arugula with parmesan shavings, 82
    baby spring, 32
    beet and goat cheese, 142
    blueberry and arugula, 70
    calamari, in pesto oil, 130
    caprese, 94, 174, 175
    corn and tomato, 114
    farro, with olives and pink grapefruit,
        45
    goat cheese, with endive and
        cucumber, 198
    Greek, big fat, 104
    Italian chopped, 128
    pizza toppings, 210
    potato, red, white and blue, 116
    the stand up, 176
salad dressing
    creamy Italian, 70, 198
    lemon-shallot vinaigrette, 32
    thyme and rice vinegar, 116
    thyme-lime, 142
salmon, grilled whole, 96
salsa verde, 58
sandwiches
    grilled brie, 187

ice cream, homemade chocolate chip,
    154
sangria, limoncello, 174
sauce
    arrabbiata, 94
    basil cream, 174
    chermoula, 186
    coconut sour cream, 58
    kumquat cranberry, 166
    pizza topping, 210
    raspberry, 36, 48
    red pepper aioli, 177
    strawberry, 178–179
    tomato, for shrimp "cocktails," 176–177
    tomato–red pepper coulis, 130
    tzatziki, 104
sausage and peppers, 188
seafood. See also shrimp
    calamari salad in pesto oil, 130
    mussels in white wine, 92
    pasta frutti di mare, 128
self-service, 60, 104, 167, 187, 210
serving pieces. See elements
shooters, grilled pea soup, 68
shrimp
    "cocktails," lemony risotto, 176–177
    and grits, white, 200
    pasta frutti di mare, 128
    and tomatoes, herb-roasted, 131
slaw, cucumber, 104
snack mix, big game, 208
sorbet, Campari-orange, 132
soufflés, apple cheddar, 198
soup
    acorn squash, 162
    chilled gazpacho, 57
    grilled pea shooters, 69
    roasted chicken noodle, 186
    white bean and kale, 142
    white bean vegetable farro, 186
sour cream, coconut, 58
spa parties, 101

spa water, 106
spaghettini with zucchini coins, speck and truffle oil, 82
spring garden parties. See also Cinco de Mayo parties; Easter lunch; Italian spring feast; Memorial Day cookout
    about, 27
    elements of, 27, 30, 32, 34, 36, 39
    menu for, 29–36
squash
    blossoms, ricotta-stuffed fried, 77, 80–81
    soup, acorn, 162
steak, grilled flank, 72
storage, 214
strawberry
    sauce, 178–179
    tiramisu, 98
    trifle, 48
stuffing
    lemon and herb, 46
    pear, walnut and bacon, 164
styling, 8, 16. See also elements
summer pool grill-out. See also Fourth of July picnic; Italian spring feast; Palio celebration; retro Riviera parties
    about, 101
    elements, 104, 105, 107, 108
    menu, 103–106
Sunday supper
    about, 149
    elements, 149, 152, 154, 156
    menu, 149, 150–154
supplies, 13–23. See also elements
sweet potato oven fries, 106

t

table runners, 94, 108, 118, 144, 192, 215
tablecloths, 27, 41, 52, 64, 82, 202
tacos, soft, Coca-Cola ancho chile pulled brisket, 60
takeaway food, 120, 151, 166, 171, 178, 180, 192
tapenade, olive, 30, 210
textiles. See elements
texture, 27, 55
Thanksgiving celebration
    about, 159
    elements, 159, 163, 164, 168–169
    menu, 161–166
thyme
    lime dressing, 142
    and rice vinegar dressing, 116
    simple syrup, 126
tiramisu, strawberry, 98
tomato(es)
    arrabbiata sauce, 94
    caprese salad, 94, 174, 175
    grilled whole salmon with lemon, zucchini and, 96
    herb-roasted shrimp and, 131
    jam, 94
    red pepper coulis, 130
    salad, corn and, 114
    salsa verde, 58
    sauce, for shrimp "cocktails," 176–177
    sun-dried, and olive bread, 151
    sun-dried, marinade, 72
tortilla chips, sweet, 62
trifle, individual fruit, 48
trout, grilled whole rainbow, 34
truffle oil
    popcorn, 178
    spaghettini with zucchini coins, speck and, 82
turkey, roast, 164
Tuscan sweet and sour kale, 44
tzatziki lamb burgers, mini, 104

v

vegetable(s). See also specific vegetables
    bruschetta, grilled, 43
    gravy, roasted, 164

pizza topping, 210
soup, white bean farro, 186
vinaigrette, lemon-shallot, 32

w

walnut, pear and bacon stuffing, 164
white bean
    chili, 188
    and kale soup, 142
    vegetable farro soup, 186
white parties
    about, 195
    elements of, 195, 198, 202–203
    menu for, 195, 197–200
wine
    limoncello sangria, 174
    tasting, 92, 137
    white, mussels in, 92
wine harvest parties
    about, 137
    elements of, 140, 142, 144, 146
    menu for, 139–142, 145
winter. See comfort food get-togethers; game day pizza parties; holiday cocktail open house; white parties

z

zucchini
    grilled whole salmon with lemon, tomatoes and, 96
    spaghettini with speck and truffle oil, 82

SOURCE GUIDE

TABLETOP + DÉCOR

ABC CARPETS
Plates, glasses, linens
www.abchome.com
(646) 602-3797

ANTHROPOLOGIE
Plates, linens, flatware, glasses
www.anthropologie.com
(800) 309-2500

BALLARD DESIGNS
Platters, glasses, spa water oversized jar,
marble cake stands
www.ballarddesigns.com
(800) 536-7551

BHLDN
Place cards and holders, felt leaves, small
takeaway bags
www.bhldn.com
(888) 942-4536

C'EST MOI
Linens, plates, glasses, serveware
www.cestmoihome.com
(770) 977-8468

CRATE & BARREL
Linens, plates, glasses, flatware, vases,
platters, candleholders
www.crateandbarrel.com
(800) 967-6696

DONNA HAY AUSTRALIA
Enamelware
www.donnahay.com.au

DUNES AND DUCHESS
Grey candelabra in the Retro Riviera Party
www.dunesandduchess.com

ERIKA READE LTD
Linens, plates, wooden spreaders, cheese servers
www.erikareadeltd.com
(404) 233-3857

EUROPE 2 YOU
Wooden cutting boards, cutting boards with
numbers, flatware, espresso cups, plates,
oversize apothecary jars, metal folding table
www.europe2you.com
(770) 998-7175

FISHS EDDY
Cake stands, plates, tea towels
www.fishseddy.com
(877) 347-4733

HAYNEEDLE.COM
Garden string lights, plates, glasses

www.hayneedle.com
(888) 880-4884

HOMEGOODS
Plates, glasses, vases
www.homegoods.com
(800) 952-5133

HOME MINT
Linens, ceramics, black linen tablecloth,
black-and-white pitcher
www.homemint.com
(888) 556-9631

IKEA
Plates, paper napkins, jars
www.ikea.com
(888) 888-4532

MERCI-PARIS (FRANCE)
Linens, gift tags
www.merci-merci.com

PIECES
Wooden art piece, white free-form wine glasses
www.piecesinc.com
(404) 869-2477

POTTERY BARN
Candles, candleholders, votives, trays
www.potterybarn.com
(888) 779-5176

STAR PROVISIONS
Glasses, linens, plates, galvanized cake plates
www.starprovisions.com
(404) 365-0410

TARGET
Plastic bowls, plastic plates, colorful
duct tape
www.target.com
(800) 591-3869

WAYFAIR
Bakeware, candles, linens, pizza stone
www.wayfair.com
(877) 929-3247

WEST ELM
Linens, plates, candle holders
www.westelm.com
(888) 922-4119

WORLD MARKET
Bowls, casseroles, trays, platters, paper
pom-poms and paper garlands, ornaments,
bottle brush Christmas trees, burlap
lampshades, slice of tree trunk
www.worldmarket.com
(877) 967-5362

Z GALLERIE
Geometric pouf ottomans, martini glasses,

highball glasses
www.zgallerie.com
(800) 908-6748

FABRIC + TEXTILES

HABLE CONSTRUCTION
Fabric for runner and napkins
www.hableconstruction.com
(817) 422-5313

HANCOCK FABRICS
Fabric
www.hancockfabrics.com

ICE MILK APRONS
Apron for Thanksgiving
www.icemilkaprons.com
(866) 486-3622

CRAFTS + PAPER + PAINT + HARDWARE

AMAZON.COM
Beach balls, paper pom-poms, pipettes
www.amazon.com

CONTAINER STORE
Jars, ribbon, tags
www.containerstore.com
(888) 266-8246

FARMHOUSE WARES
Galvanized cake plates
www.farmhousewares.com
(866) 567-7958

HOBBY LOBBY
Fabric, ribbon, moss, bags of snow-globe snow
www.hobbylobby.com
(800) 888-0321

HOME DEPOT
Wood, chalkboard paint
www.homedepot.com
(800) 466-3337

MICHAELS
Raffia, jute twine, ribbon, cupcake liners, paper
bags, stick-on letters, gift tags, stick-on tags
www.michaels.com
(800) 642-4235

PAPER SOURCE
Card stock, envelopes, wrapping paper, ribbon,
washi tape, butcher's string, gift tags, paper
table runner
www.paper-source.com
(888) 727-3711

SAM FLAX
Craft paper, ribbon, twine, stickers
www.samflaxsouth.com
(800) 726-3529

VINTAGE + ANTIQUES

EBAY
Vintage Thermoses
www.ebay.com

ETSY
Mid-century juice glasses, enamel casserole
www.etsy.com

INNER PIECES
Glass beakers, antique tables, antique chairs,
antique books, ironstone, antique flatware
Lisa Burnett, innerpieces@aol.com
(404) 808-7135

REBEL RECLAIMED
Vintage blankets, Thermoses, and lanterns
www.rebelreclaimed.com
(616) 218-9257

ROSWELL ANTIQUES MARKET
Burlap bags, glasses, pewter, ironstone
www.roswellantiques.com
(770) 587-5259

KITCHEN RETAILERS

CIRCULON COOKWARE
Soup pots, knives
www.circulon.com
(800) 326-3933

SUR LA TABLE
Linens, Moka espresso pot, flavored oils,
paella pan
www.surlatable.com

WILLIAMS-SONOMA
Linens, plates, bowls, glasses, soufflé dishes,
casseroles, platters
www.williams-sonoma.com
(877) 812-6235

FOOD + GOURMET SPECIALTY STORES

AMAZON.COM
Snap organic liqueur
www.amazon.com

O & CO.
Lemon and Mandarin-infused olive oils
www.oliviersandco.com
(877) 828-6620

FLOWERS + PLANTS

CUT FLOWERS WHOLESALE
Fresh flowers, plants, and glass vases
www.cutflower.com
(404) 320-1619